Hecate
The Witches' Goddess

By Gary R. Varner
Member American Folklore Society

ISBN: 978-1-257-06020-7 (paperback)
Also available in Kindle Editions

An OakChylde Book published by Lulu Press, Inc.
Visit the author's website: www.authorsden.com/garyrvarner

Title page illustration: Stephane Mallarmé
Les Dieux Antiques, nouvelle mythologie illustrée. Paris, 1880.

Contents

Like the bow and arrow of the twins, Hekate's magic can be made to strike far from home. –Nor Hall *The Moon and The Virgin*

I saw a fearsome woman approaching me, almost half a stadium's length high. In her left hand she held a torch and in her right a sword twenty cubits long. Below the waist she had snake-feet, above it she resembled a Gorgon… --from the 2nd century Greek text *Philopseuedes* by Lucian

Introduction

Hecate, goddess of witches, magic and the underworld. Feared and worshipped for thousands of years by many cultures around the world, known by several names and credited with many powers.

Like most ancient gods and goddesses, Hecate's story has changed over time. Originally, a goddess of wilderness and childbirth, she eventually became known as "Queen of Ghosts." Her origins may be in Asia Minor among the Carians or in North Africa in the Nubian kingdom.

The Hecate sanctuary at Lagina, Turkey. One of the major sacred sites of ancient Anatolia. (Photo source: Municipality of Turgut)

Later she was worshipped by the Greeks and appeared in Homer's Hymn to Demeter and in *Theogony* ("The Birth of Gods") by Hesiod.

Hesiod was deeply enamored of the goddess as illustrated in this portion from *Theogony:*

"Then the goddess through the love of the god conceived and brought forth dark-gowned Leto, always mild, kind to men and to the deathless gods, mild from the beginning, gentlest in all Olympus. Also she bare Asteria of happy name, whom Perses once led to his great house to be called his dear wife. And she conceived and bare Hecate whom Zeus the son of Cronos honoured above all. He gave her splendid gifts, to have a share of the earth and the unfruitful sea. She received honour also in starry heaven, and is honoured exceedingly by the deathless gods. For to this day, whenever any one of men on earth offers rich sacrifices and prays for favour according to custom, he calls upon Hecate. Great honour comes full easily to him whose prayers the goddess receives favourably, and she bestows wealth upon him; for the power surely is with her. For as many as were born of Earth and Ocean amongst all these she has her due portion. The son of Cronos did her no wrong nor took anything away of all that was her portion among the former Titan gods: but she holds, as the division was at the first from the beginning, privilege both in earth, and in heaven, and in sea. Also, because she is an only child, the goddess receives not less honour, but much more still, for Zeus honours her. Whom she will she greatly aids and advances: she sits by worshipful kings in judgement, and in the assembly whom she will is distinguished among the people.

And when men arm themselves for the battle that destroys men, then the goddess is at hand to give victory and grant glory readily to whom she will. Good is she also when men contend at the games, for there too the goddess is with them and profits them: and he who by might and strength gets the victory wins the rich prize easily with joy, and brings glory to his parents. And she is good to stand by horsemen, whom she will: and to those whose business is in the grey discomfortable sea, and who pray to Hecate and the loud-crashing Earth-Shaker, easily the glorious goddess gives great catch, and easily she takes it away as soon as seen, if so she will. She is good in the byre with Hermes to increase the stock. The droves of kine and wide herds of goats and flocks of fleecy sheep, if she will, she increases from a few, or makes many to be less. So, then. albeit her mother's only child (17), she is honoured amongst all the deathless gods. And the son of Cronos made her a nurse of the young who after that day saw with their eyes the light of all-seeing Dawn. So from the beginning she is a nurse of the young, and these are her honours." [1]

She was recognized as a Great Goddess from Asia Minor to Thrace to Macedonia and Greece. Strangely enough, she has been compared to the Norse goddess of the underworld Hel, the Egyptian Mother Goddess Isis and to the Virgin Mary. Her dual nature apparent in the comparisons.

---

[1] The Theogony of Hesiod translated by Hugh G. Evelyn-White [1914]. Mineola: Dover Publications 2006 reprint of the 1914 edition.

For the most part Hecate is seen today as the Goddess of Witches and Sorcery—but this wasn't always so. Hecate was at one time both protectress of women and children and Goddess of Death. She was, in her trinity aspect, goddess of fertility and prosperity, Goddess of the Moon, and Queen of Ghosts, shades and the night. It is interesting that she was seen both as the goddess of fertility and life as well as death.

"Hekate can poison as well as intoxicate," wrote Nor Hall, "turn ecstasy into madness, and cause death where incubation—or a short journey—was intended."

This book will examine her many facets and bring about a truer sense of the primal goddess known as "The Distant One" and "The Nameless One." One of her titles places these in a softer light, for she was also called "most lovely one."

One
The Nature of Hecate – Who is this Goddess?

Contrary to popular Neo-Pagan literature, Hecate was much more than a Dark Goddess focused purely on death and sorcery. As with many divine figures her nature changed as time progressed. Each age viewed her in a manner which was comfortable to the time and fit the current societal view. Her origins most likely were in North Africa as her name appears in early Nubian texts and next she appears in Egypt as Heqat.

Hecate was an only child, born to the star-goddess Asteria, a virgin Titan (for many gods and goddesses were born of virgin mothers). Zeus destroyed the Titans however; he held Hecate in great respect and allowed her to live on. According to myth, she was born fully formed and powerful on the earth as well as in the heavens and under the seas. Her mother was the creatress known as the Queen of Heaven. Hecate was, according to Michael Stapleton, "one who retained her great powers for good in the fortunes of mankind." [2] To be fair Hecate was an earth-goddess and so connected to the dead and the underworld. In addition, she is goddess of the dark of the moon who is not only the destroyer of life but also the restorer of life. But she was much more than the Dark Goddess sought after by sorcerers.

---

[2] Stapleton, Michael. *Library of the World's Myths and Legends: Greek and Roman Mythology.* New York: Peter Bedrick Books 1986, 89.

One of her many aspects was the Queen of the Elfin or Faerie—this in Scotland. She was also recognized in Medieval South Wales as the mother of nine "wild women" who terrorized any male caught trespassing in their territory.

Hecate was a triune goddess well known as the goddess of crossroads and protector of entrances. In many ways, she was similar to the Roman god Janus who was also regarded as the opener and fastener of all things. Both gods were able to see the past as well as the future.

The Greeks set poles at every three-way crossroad with masks of Hecate in her triune role facing in each direction. Her role as goddess of the crossroads undoubtedly originated in her ancient position as goddess of the wilderness and the untamed land. This practice is also similar to the erection of posts with the likeness of Hermes which marked boundaries. These posts, or rather columns, were called *hermaii* and were described as "simple columns tapering towards the ground and surmounted by a head of the god. From the centre of the column an erect phallus protruded…giving…the Greeks a feeling of reassurance…" [3]

Hermes, like Hecate, was regarded as a pastoral deity linked to the Earth and to fertility in both humans and animals. And, like Hecate, his association with the earth linked him as well to death. As Buffie

[3] Ibid, 104.

Johnson noted, "It seems inevitable that Hermes, the messenger to the underworld, would meet Hecate and fall in love with her."[4]

Hermes shared many things in common with Hecate, including skill in sorcery and a close association with dogs.

Hecate and Hermes had a child, Circe, who was skilled in enchantment like her parents. Circe, the Moon Goddess, passed her knowledge on to her niece Medea.

Goddess of the Crossroads

Hecate was foremost the goddess and guardian of the crossroads. One reason for this is the belief in ancient times that crossroads, above all other places, were haunted at midnight, as they were places where the dead gathered. Travelers would offer sacrifice to her at these locations to assure their safe transit. She was known to look in the three directions at crossroads at the same time.

According to legend, it was believed that Hecate would appear in the intersection of crossroads on clear nights in the company of her dogs and supernatural beings. Sacrifices were placed at crossroads not only to ask Hecate for safe passage, but to ask for her help to avoid madness which was believed to be caused by wondering souls. Part of this fear may have been caused by a darker use of the crossroads other than travel. According to Cooper, "Burials of suicides, vampires and felons at crossroads ensured their confusion of ways and prevented

---

[4] Johnson, Buffie. *Lady of the Beasts: The Goddess and Her Sacred Animals.* Rochester: Inner Traditions International 1994, 160.

their return to haunt the living." [5] They obviously were confined to the crossroads to haunt.

Due to this fearsome use of the crossroads as well as their association with Hecate, they were viewed as places where sorcery was performed as well as where pacts with Satan were made. Russell speaks of one woman's confession to charges of witchcraft during the Middle Ages:

"Catherine Delort confessed that ten years previously she had an affair with a shepherd who had persuaded her to make a pact with Satan. He took her at midnight to a crossroads at the edge of a forest. There they built a fire, putting on it the remains of human bodies they had taken from a cemetery. She cut her left arm and let a few drops of her blood fall onto the burning mess, while speaking strange words which she did not now remember. Thereupon a demon named Berit appeared in the shape of a purplish flame, which evidently conferred upon her the power to do all kinds of maleficium." [6] Catherine Delort was given over to the secular authorities and burned after implicating others as witches.

Why does something that is viewed as a traverse between worlds looked upon with fear and trepidation? It isn't because of Hecate, as she is actually the guardian of the gateway. Most likely it is because of

---

[5] Cooper, J.C. *An Illustrated Encyclopaedia of Traditional Symbols.* London: Thames and Hudson Ltd. 1978, 46.

[6] Russell, Jeffrey Burton. *Witchcraft in the Middle Ages.* Ithaca: Cornell University Press 1972, 184

the horrible things that man has done to man at these places to create an atmosphere of dread, to cause the souls of the punished to linger where they died, to cause man to invoke a guardian goddess to protect him as he crosses the pathway.

However, the tradition of Hecate survived for hundreds and thousands of years—along with those of her dogs. "The Highland witches in the eighteenth century," wrote Margaret Murray, "saw the devil as a dog; he was 'a large black ugly tyke', to whom the witches made obeisance; the dog acknowledged the homage 'by bowing, grinning, and clapping his paws." [7]

Hecate herself was referred to as the "Black she-dog." She was also described thusly: "They say that she was excessive tall, her Head was covered with frightful Snakes instead of Hair, and her Feet were like Serpents."[8]

In addition, Hecate was, according to Howey, "Diana on earth" whose priestesses were to become the later witches. [9]

Barbara Walker wrote that Hecate was "One of the oldest Greek versions of the Trinitarian Goddess…derived from the Egyptian midwife-goddess Heqit, Heket, or Hekat, who in turn evolved from

[7] Murray, Margaret A. *The Witch-Cult in Western Europe.* Oxford: Oxford University Press 1921, 68.
[8] Quoted by M. Oldfield Howey in *The Cat in Magic, Mythology, and Religion.* New York: Crescent Books 1989, 21.
[9] Ibid., 86.

the *heq* or tribal matriarch of pre-dynastic Egypt: a wise-woman, in command of all the *herkau* or 'mother's Words of Power.'" [10]

There is no doubt that Hecate was a "foreign" goddess, ancient before her advent into Greek culture. Her arrival in Greek religion was not an easy transition as many of the roles that she filled were already occupied by important goddesses in the Greek pantheon—such as Artemis. Originally a Mother Goddess, Hecate changed as her cult grew.

The mythology surrounding Hecate indicates this gradual change in her stature. Early myth tells of Hecate as a mortal priestess who commits suicide. After her death, the goddess Artemis adorns Hecate's body with jewels and whispers to her to rise up—to become the goddess Hecate. In this way, the Greek myths allow the foreign goddess into the pantheon purely on the basis of being "adopted" by a primal Greek deity. As her followers grew and her cult became more important other myths were created for Hecate, including the birth of Zeus and Hecate's role in protecting the infant god.

There are strong indications that Hecate was a Nubian-Egyptian goddess—the most important of the Egyptian deities, not only as Heqat but as Isis.

Second century Roman author Apuleius wrote a lengthy, possibly autobiographical, piece in his book, *Metamorphoses*, or *The Golden Ass* about a convert to Isis. Isis addresses the convert:

---

[10] Walker, Barbara G. *The Woman's Encyclopedia of Myths and Secrets.* Edison: Castle Books 1996, 378.

"In one land the Phrygians, first-born of men, hail me as the Pessinuntian mother of the gods; elsewhere the native dwellers of Attica call me Cecropian Minerva; in other climes the wave-tossed Cypriots name me Paphian Venus; the Cretan archers, Dictynna Diana; the trilingual Sicilians, Ortygian Proserpina; the Eleusians, the ancient goddess Ceres; some call me Juno, other Bellona, others Hecate, and others still Rhamnusia. But the peoples on whom the rising sun-god shines with his first rays—eastern and western Ethiopians, and the Egyptians who flourish with their time-honoured learning—worship me with the liturgy that is my own, and call me by my true name, which is queen Isis." [11]

[11] As quoted in *Women's Religions in the Greco-Roman World: A Sourcebook.* Edited by Ross Shepard Kraemer. Oxford: Oxford University Press 2004, 440.

Hecate's Wheel

The Strophalos, or Hecate's wheel is an ancient Greek symbol described in the 2nd century Alexandrian text, the *Chaldean Oracal.* It represents the goddess's threefold nature

Two
The Goddess of Death, Witchcraft and Magic

Hecate, overtime, became the witches' goddess. This was inevitable due to her association with death and her link with the darkening moon. Legends of her are horrifying. Some speak of her roaming the earth with her pack of red-eyed hounds and her followers of the souls of the dead. She was said to wear a necklace of testicles and her hair a writhing mass of serpents, much as Medusa's. Reportedly, only dogs were able to see her in the night, howling their announcement of her passing by. She was the making of nightmares and the cause of insanity.

It was primarily during the Middle Ages that Hecate was labeled Queen of the Ghostworld and Queen of Witches. Walker noted "She was especially diabolized by Catholic authorities who said people most dangerous to the faith were precisely those whom Hecate patronized: the midwives. Her ancient threefold power was copied, however, by priestly writers who reassigned it to their own deity: 'The threefold power of Christ, namely in Heaven, in earth, and in Hell.'"[12]

While Walker is correct in her statement, Hecate was recognized as a powerful goddess over life and death and was often invoked by those that we would all recognize as sorcerers.

---

[12] Walker, Barbara G. *The Women's Encyclopedia of Myths and Secrets.* Edison: Castle Books 1996, 379.

Hecate had a dual nature—as do most gods, goddesses and symbols of humankind. She destroyed life but also restored life. She was certainly respected in the ancient past as statues of her carrying swords or torches were erected outside of homes to protect them and images of her were also erected at the crossroads where people would perform certain rituals of appeasement to her. Offerings of honey cakes, chicken hearts, onions, eggs and fish were left at the crossroads on the last day of the month along with more grisly sacrifices of black puppies and, according to some, infant girls and she-lambs.

Over time sorcerers gathered at these locations to not only pay homage to Hecate, but also to other supernatural beings such as a hobgoblin called Empusa, a poltergeist and a ghoul by the name of Mormo. [13] It should be noted, however, that Hecate was not only worshipped by sorcerers but also by those who sought her protection against evil.

An early invocation to Hecate recorded in a 3rd century manuscript called *Philosophumena* reads:

"Come infernal, terrestrial, and celestial Bombo, goddess of the cross-roads, guiding light, queen of the night, enemy of the sun, and friend and companion of the darkness; you who rejoice to hear the barking of dogs and to see blood flow; you who wander among the tombs in the hours of darkness, thirsty for blood, and the terror of

---

[13] Guiley, Rosemary Ellen. *The Encyclopedia of Witches & Witchcraft.* New York: Checkmark Books 1999, 154.

mortal men; Gorgo, Mormo, moon of a thousand forms, look favorably on my sacrifice."

According to Elworthy, Hecate was the inventor of the art of pharmacy—or rather herbal drugs. "To this great art of pharmacy," he wrote, "belong all the charms, amulets, and enchantments against poison, venom of serpents, with all diseases; and hence of course our modern use of the word." [14]

As goddess of the dark moon, Hecate was the ruler of the dead. In fact she was married to Hades. She was also known as the controller of ghostly swarms that scavenged the streets and crossroads. She was arbiter of souls and bringer of death. Evening meals were often dedicated to her and any leftovers were left outside as an offering to her. Ritually prepared meals, called Hecate Suppers, were left at the intersection of crossroads as well to, as James notes, "placate her if and when she appeared with her hounds of hell." [15]

However, she had another side besides that of destroyer—she was the bringer of rain and restorer of life, she was a pastoral goddess. She was present when the soul entered the body at conception and she was present when the soul left the body at death. She represented the cyclical nature of existence, which could hardly be evil, dark or threatening but has become so after two thousand years of Christian domination. The dark moon was also more than a dreadful,

---

[14] Elworthy, Frederick Thomas. *The Evil Eye: An Account of this Ancient and Widespread Superstition.* London: John Murray 1895, 446.

[15] James, E.O. *The Cult of the Mother-Goddess.* New York: Barnes & Noble, Inc. 1994, 153.

threatening image as it was linked with divination, healing and illumination. "So the Dark Goddess," wrote Monica Sjöö and Barbara Mor, "presided over love-magic, metamorphosis, wonder-working, and medicinal healing." [16]

Hecate was also considered the nurturer of children, which is certainly in contradiction to her image as a deity that had infants sacrificed to her. In Hesiod's *Theogony*, however, she was "endowed with frightening magical powers exercised in sorcery." [17]

Hecate's reputation as a goddess of sorcery and witchcraft is due to several things. First, Hecate is credited with the "invention" or herbal potions which could cure as well as kill. Medea, who figures in the mythic tales of Jason, was an enchanter, niece to Circe and priestess to Hecate. Medea was also a witch. She used sorcery to "stay the course of rivers" and to "check the paths of the stars and the moon." She also used magical herbal concoctions to kill.

Second, Hecate was well known as the Queen of Ghosts and guardian of the underworld who resided in tombs and graveyards waiting for the souls of the dead. As goddess of the crossroads, Hecate was invoked to provide protection against evil spirits. Statues of her were placed not only at these crossroads but also at the doorways of homes to provide the same protection. However, in time it was felt

---

[16] Sjöö, Monica and Barbara Mor. *The Great Cosmic Mother: Rediscovering the Religion of the Earth.* San Francisco: HarperSanFrancisco 1991, 183.
[17] James, op cit., 152.

that if Hecate became offended she could also let these evil spirits in as well as keep them out.

During the witch trials of the Middle Ages, many were burned as witches because of their shamanic, ecstatic religious practices. Such practices were, according to 19th century researcher F.J. Mone, "derived from the Greek cults of Hecate and Dionysus through contacts made by Germanic tribes who populated the north coast of the Black Sea. The tribes had absorbed what we would now call Shamanic practice and belief into a cult which worshipped the Horned God and practiced magic." [18] These shamanic religions survived well into Medieval times and their followers were those hunted down and murdered as Satanic witches.

King James I, "defender of the faith" and, according to Howey "the famous British demonologist," made a concerted effort to eradicate "the fragmentary and degraded survivals of the once noble, profoundly occult religion of Diana Triforms"—Hecate. [19]

Howey went on to say "it was Hecate alone that the uninitiated, irreverent bigots glimpsed the threefold goddess when they sought to tear aside the veil that covered her…the bitter persecution instigated by the Christian churches, brought forth further distortion and concealment of its true tenets." [20]

---

[18] Crowley, Vivianne. *Phoenix and the Flame: Pagan Spirituality in the Western World.* London: Aquarian/Thorsons 1994, 100.
[19] Howey, M. Oldfield. *The Cat in Magic, Mythology, and Religion.* New York: Crescent Books 1989, 88.
[20] Ibid.

Archaeological excavations over time have shown that Hecate was absorbed by the Christian Church in some ways. At Bouches-du-Rhône, France [21] one of Christianity's mysterious "Black Virgins" was found at the site of an ancient sanctuary dedicated to Hecate. The Black Virgins have long perplexed scholars as to what they actually represented and it is possible that they are, in fact, directly tied to Hecate. As the Dark Goddess, what better legacy than to become the Black Virgin? However, this theory cannot be proven. Christians, if they did not outright destroy ancient temples and shrines of the Old Religion, often replaced or absorbed pagan images and sacred sites with Christian ones.

As goddess of the underworld and often invoked to provide justice Hecate was used in ritual and spell work to exact retribution. By using of the term "spell work," I mean that they used invocations and curses to attempt to persuade the gods to give them what they desired.

Deities often addressed included not only Hecate, but Hades, Hermes, Persephone, Demeter and Gaia. The Furies were also invoked as they were regarded as "the avengers of those that died by violence."[22]

---

[21] Markale, Jean. *The Great Goddess.* Rochester: Inner Traditions 19990, 253.
[22] Ogden, Daniel. "Binding Spells: Curse Tablets and Voodoo Dolls in the Greek and Roman World" in *Witchcraft and Magic in Europe: Ancient Greece and Rome.* Ed. by Bengt Ankarloo and Stuart Clark. Philadelphia: University of Pennsylvania Press 1999, 44.

One of the earliest documented instances of the use of Hecate's name in a curse is from the 5th century BCE. Found near Mycenae it reportedly was written to give thanks for an act of retribution:

"The Ephesian vengeance was sent down. Firstly, Hecate harms the belongings of Megara in all things, and then Persephone reports to the gods. All these things are already so." [23]

Another text, dating from the 3rd century BCE, is that of *Idyll 2, The Witch* by Theocritus. Written as a spell to recover a lover, the abandoned Simaetha invokes Hecate in an effort to empower potions to do their work and to reclaim her lover Delphis:

"Welcome, frightful Hecate, and accompany me to the completion of my task. Render these drugs no less powerful that those of Circe, Medea, or blonde Perimede." [24]

Using sympathetic, love and erotic magic, the girl is reunited with Delphis and gives thanks to the goddess: "Goodbye, lady, turn your horses toward Ocean….Goodbye Moon of the shining throne, goodbye, you other stars, attendants of quiet Night's chariot." [25]

Other invocations were recorded to cause women sleeplessness so that they could only think of a jilted suitor or, in an early 2nd century CE text by the Greek Lucian, to open the gates of hell. In this tale, the speaker desires to enter hell to determine the secret of life. The speaker

---

[23] Ibid., 47.

[24] Ogden, Daniel. *Magic, Witchcraft, and Ghosts in the Greek and Roman Worlds: A Sourcebook.* Oxford: Oxford University Press 2002, 108.

[25] Ibid. 111.

has fooled a ferryman to take him across the Tigris to the land of the dead.

"We crossed this and came to a deserted place, wooded and sunless. Here we disembarked and...dug a pit, jugulated the sheep (as offerings), and libated their blood around it. Meanwhile the mage, holding up his torch, shouted out at the top of his voice, using his subdued tone no longer, and invoked all the demons together, the Poenae, the Furies, 'Hecate of the night and dead Persephone...' and he missed in some meaningless foreign names and polysyllables.

"At once the whole area shook and the ground was broken open by the spell. One could hear the barking of Cerberus in the distance, and everything looked dismal and gloomy..." [26]

It was during the 2nd century as well that these spells, these invocations began to change. Strong Jewish influence was incorporated into the spells with a Judeo-Christian mixing with pagan spell craft. One of these, called a Megarian prayer for justice, reads thusly:

"...we devote them to evil. Althaea, Kore, Oreobazagra, Hecate the tail-eating, Moon. ..we devote these people to evil, body, spirit, soul, intellect, reflection, perception, life, with Hecataean words and Hebraic oaths...justice...Earth. Hecate...under the command of the holy names and the Hebraic oaths..." [27]

---

[26] Ibid., 186.
[27] Ibid., 222.

Obviously the powers of Hecate were not forsaken by the reportedly monotheistic religions of Judaism and Christianity. Perhaps they believed it better to be safe than sorry in the endeavors.

An early sculptural depiction of Hecate,
Triple Hecate and the Charites, Attic, 3rd century BCE (Glyptothek, Munich)

Three
Hecate, the Triune Goddess

As previously mentioned, Hecate is the guardian of the crossroads and gatekeeper to the underworld. She was able to view three directions at once in her triune nature of Hecate, Selene and Diana/Artemis. She is the lunar Triple Goddess and is often depicted in the maiden/mother/crone aspect.

Many of the ancient images of Hecate show her in this triple-goddess role. However, the earliest Greek depictions of her show her as a single faced woman—not tri-faced. The earliest known sculpture of Hecate is a small terracotta statue found in Athens. Dating from the 6th century BCE, this statue is rather plain and ordinary and the only indication that it represents a goddess at all is the inscription of Hecate's name. The first tri-form depiction was created in the 5th century BCE by the sculpture Alkamenes. Many of the early tri-form sculptures show Hecate at three individuals rather than one figure with three faces. It is probable that the evolution of the tri-form sculpture followed the evolution of religious attitudes towards Hecate as not only an important individual goddess but a goddess representing three realms—that of the moon, the earth and the sea.

This triune nature given to Hecate was probably due to a amalgamation of goddesses by the Greeks. In speaking about the goddess Artemis, 19th century mythologist Talfourd Ely wrote,

"…Artemis has had to allow herself to be blended with another deity essentially foreign, who was glorified as queen of the three kingdoms if Earth, Air, and Water. In air she ruled as goddess of the moon, and as such the Greeks called her by the old name of the moon-goddess Hekate, or the distant one. Since this moon-goddess was thought to be accompanied by dogs, it was not out of the way to interchange her with the hunting-goddess Artemis, who was equally accompanied by dogs; besides the name Hekate reminded people of Apollo Hekatebolos (the 'Far-striker')." [28] Ely notes also that the "mistress of the lower world, Persephone" was also blended into the mix.

Her relationship to Artemis is somewhat cloudy as some refer to her as the cousin of Artemis and not simply another persona of the same goddess.

[28] Ely, Talfourd. *The Gods of Greece and Rome.* Mineola: Dover Publications, Inc. 2003, 141-142.

An ancient Celtic carving of the threefold goddess.

The triple goddesses of the moon are Selene, Hecate and Diana. Diana symbolizes the new moon with its positive aspects and rules the earth, Selene rules over the full-moon and the sky and was often invoked to solve problems and was believed to represent creation. Hecate, who ruled over the dark moon and the underworld, was sought after for her powers of justice and wisdom. Hecate has three aspects as well in this trinity. She is goddess of fertility and abundance; goddess of the moon, and queen of the night and the creatures, both earthly and supernatural, that inhabit the night.

In folklore women believed, at one time, that pregnancy could be caused by moonbeams and they would sleep under the open sky to increase their fertility. Today the effects of the full moon are still felt with erratic, lunatic behavior attributed to it. However, the true powers of the moon were wielded by Hecate as it was her moon phase that slipped into the underworld which connected the land of the dead with that of the living.

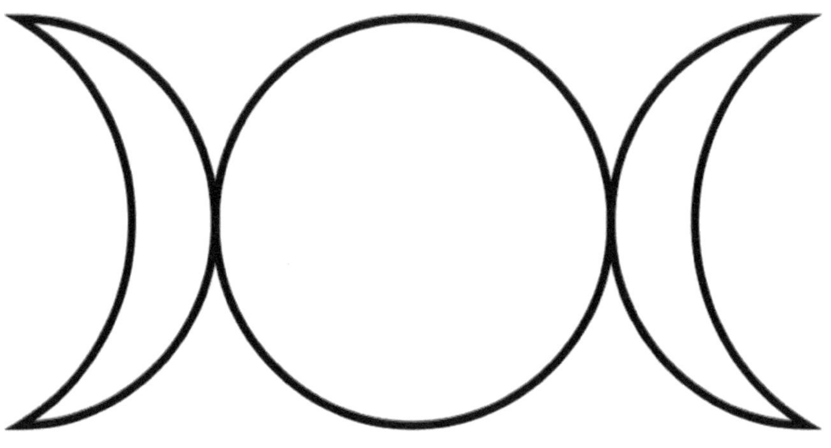

Symbol of the Triple Moon Goddess aspect of Hecate

Four
Sacred Sites of Hecate

Hecate had many temples and sanctuaries dedicated to her across the pagan world. Some of these are:

- Agrigente, Sicily where three sanctuaries dedicated to Demeter existed. Because Hecate and Demeter were closely linked in myth it is likely that Hecate was worshipped here as well.
- Baia, near Naples. This was a Temple of Diana which also contained a sacred enclosure to Hecate.
- Delos, Greece. Sanctuaries dedicated to the goddesses Artemis, Demeter, Aphrodite, and Hera. As Diana/Artemis were synonymous with Hecate it is likely that she was worshipped here as well.
- Eleusis, Greece. Sanctuary of Demeter located here where the Eleusian Mysteries took place. Again, Hecate likely was worshipped here.
- Noves, Boushes-de-Rhône, France. Sanctuary of Hecate and site of a Black Virgin. Many sanctuaries containing the Black Virgin are found in France, Spain, Austria and Swirtzerland.
- Lagina, Turkey. This is perhaps the most important sacred site dedicated to Hecate in the ancient world.

Today Lagina is a small town in southwestern Turkey called Turgut. Until recently, the town was called Leyne, which was a continuation of its ancient name. Dating from the Bronze Age, Turgut has been continuously occupied since that time and was the most important religious center of its day. Located 11 kilometers away is the site of Stratonikeia, the ancient administrative center of this sacred complex.

Lagina, a religious site sacred to Hecate. (Photo source: Municipality of Turgut)

Lagina was a theocratic city-state with Hecate's temple served by eunuchs. Hecate served as the patron goddess of Stratonikeia, the nearby Macedonian colony.

Festivals were held here as they were elsewhere in the Greek and Roman world. The Greeks observed August 13th and November 30th as sacred festival days while the Romans dedicated the 29th of every month as sacred to Hecate.

Five
The Animals of Hecate

Hecate, like other gods of the underworld, was well known for her terrifying hounds and the underworld serpent.

The dog has long been connected to the ancient Mother Goddess, protecting her mysteries and transporting the dead to the underworld. The dog was sacred to Hecate and has a strong link with the dark moon. The three-headed dog Cerberus, guardian of the underworld, was Hecate's own beast.

Hecate and Cerberus from an ancient Greek painting.

The howling of dogs was often thought to be the announcement of Hecate's approach. Hecate is often depicted with a dogs head along with that of frogs, horses and bears. Black dogs were closely associated with Hecate and were most often sacrificed to her in purification rituals. While dog sacrifice is an ancient act it should not be assumed that it was delegated only to the pagans and their religions. Dog sacrifices and even crucifixions were performed every August 3rd through the 6th century in Christian Rome. The annual crucifixion supposedly was done to commemorate the failure of dogs to give alarm that Rome was about to be attacked.

The dog has an interesting and symbolic history of its own as "Mans best friend." These three simple words describe the most familiar of humankind's animal companions. The domesticated dog is found in every nook and cranny on the earth, from Polynesia to New Guinea to deepest Africa and Australia to the North Pole. Perhaps it is this deep felt relationship with the dog that is responsible for another aspect of the canine-human tie. The dog is one of the oldest and most powerful of the shaman's spirit helpers as well as one of the most feared supernatural entities in the world.

Dogs apparently were the most favored of sacrificial animals; recall that the hound is associated with the Wild Huntsman and the journey to the Underworld. As J.C. Cooper notes, "having been a companion in life it continues as such after death and intercedes and interprets between the dead and the gods of the underworld." [29] In fact during the 1800's in India and the Middle East it was customary to bring a dog to the bedside of an individual in the process of dying "in order that the soul may be sure of a prompt escort" [30] to the land of the dead. In addition, dogs were sacred to the Goddess Hecate, herself a ruler of the Underworld, and were often sacrificed to her. In an article in the English journal *Notes and Queries* of May 28, 1859, it was stated "Plutarch states that it was a universal Greek custom to kill a dog as a purificatory sacrifice; he adds that puppies were offered to the goddess Hecate, together with other rites of lustration; and that persons who required purification were touched with puppies…" [31]

In India, the God of the Dead, Yama, had two dogs, each with four eyes. [32] Dogs were often depicted as the guardians of the Underworld because, says White, "the dog's place lies between one world and another." [33]

To the Celts, the dog was especially esteemed and was used many times in mythology and was incorporated into the names of Celtic Gods. The 200-foot deep well at Muntham Court, in Sussex had numerous dog skeletons as well as a "votive" leg, made from clay,

---

[29] Cooper, J.C. *An Illustrated Encyclopaedia on Traditional Symbols.* London: Thames and Hudson Ltd. 1978, 52.
[30] Fiske, John. *Myths and Myth-Makers: Old Tales and Superstitions Interpreted by Comparative Mythology.* Boston: Houghton, Mifflin and Company 1881, 35.
[31] *Notes and Queries*, Vol. 7, 2nd S. (178) May 28, 1859, 431.
[32] Mackenzie, Donald A. *India Myths & Legends.* London: Studio Editions 1993, 40.
[33] White, David Gordon. *Myths of the Dog-Man.* Chicago: The University of Chicago Press 1991, 14.

indicating that the well was valued for its healing properties. In other wells, such as Coventina's, dog figurines were given to the well instead of actual animals. Dogs in early Celtic society were symbolic of both healing and death. These two symbolic aspects are reflective moreover, of the dogs' representation of rebirth and their sacrifice to wells, pits and ritual shafts is fitting.

Dogs were a food source in Hawaii in addition to providing raw materials for fishhooks, jewelry and utensils. Dogs, like pigs, were both regarded as pets and as food. Titcomb notes that dogs were also suitable offerings for female deities. "Dogs were especially appropriate as offerings to the *mo'o* gods," she writes, "spirits that lived in the water." [34]

Hutton and Merrifield note that dogs were frequently sacrificed to wells at the time of the termination of the well's use—especially during the Roman occupation of Britain. A pair of dogs was sacrificed at Farnworth in Gloucestershire during the 4th century C.E., two in Southwark dated to the 3rd century and eight pairs in a well in Surrey (along with red-deer antler, two complete dishes and a broken flagon).[35] A recent excavation at an ancient well at Shiptonthorpe in Yorkshire uncovered a number of dog skulls as well as the remains of

[34] Titcomb, Margaret. *Dog and Man in the Ancient Pacific.* Honolulu: Bernice P. Bishop Museum Special Publication 59 1969, 18.

[35] Hutton, Ronald. *The Pagan Religions of the Ancient British Isles: Their Nature and Legacy*. Oxford: Blackwell Publishers Ltd., 1991, 231 and Merrifield, Ralph. *The Archaeology of Ritual and M*agic. New York: New Amsterdam Books 1987, 47.

bundles of mistletoe. Because mistletoe was so important in Druidic rites, this well may have been an important ritual site.

Other dog sacrifices have been found in Holland, Germany and among Scandinavian Viking-age ship burials as well as in smaller individual graves, and in America. Davidson notes, "the most elaborate [dog sacrifice] example being from Mannhagen in Holland, where the skulls of twelve dogs were found with the skull of a horse and that of a man."[36] Contemporary dog sacrifice continues in Africa. Mbiti tells us "Every fortnight Yoruba blacksmiths sacrifice dogs to *Ogun* the divinity of iron and war." [37] The Iroquoise sacrificed white dogs, believing that the dead dogs spirit could intercede on their behalf with the Iroquoise gods.

Dogs were valued as healing agents also and it is interesting that the use of dog skulls to rub ointment on the swollen legs of horses and cattle continued into 17th century France. This method of healing was thought to be even more effective if the local priest had blessed the skull beforehand. [38]

Images of dogs have been painted on ancient vases found in eastern Europe guarding the Tree of Life as well as on others appearing alongside images of caterpillars signifying both death and rebirth. As previously indicated dogs also guard the land of the dead

---

[36] Davidson, H. R. Ellis. *Myths and Symbols in Pagan Europe: Early Scandinavian and Celtic Religions.* Syracuse: Syracuse University Press 1988, 57.

[37] Mbiti, John S. *African Religions and Philosophy.* Garden City: Anchor Books 1969, 78.

[38] Briggs, Robin. *Witches & Neighbors: The Social and Cultural Context of European Witchcraft.* New York: Viking Press 1996, 121.

and, as the Egyptian god, Anubis acts as the guide of souls to the Underworld. This concept is also present in the folklore of the Yupa Indians who inhabit areas between Columbia and Venezuela. According to anthropologist Johannes Wilbert, "the dog plays a vital part in guiding the dead to the next world, and to mistreat a dog would condemn its owner to wander for eternity somewhere between earth and 'heaven.'" [39]

Anubis, the dog deity of Egypt

[39] Wilbert, Johannes. *Yupa Folktales.* Latin American Studies, Volume 24. Los Angeles: University of California Los Angeles 1974, 42.

An ancient tale from New Ireland in the New Guinea chain says that dogs were originally a race of dwarfs "who were said to be very strong and active," [40] and whom the residents greatly feared. These dwarfs walked erect, ran very fast, and killed men that they overtook. Some of the Islanders cooked breadfruit seeds and laid them across the pathways that the dwarfs usually used, causing them to burn their feet and fall to their hands. According to legend, they were forever unable to walk erect again.

Dog Symbolism

The dog has been regarded as the guardian and keeper of the passageway between our physical world and that of the Underworld. The dog, often seen as a guardian of Underworld treasures, in reality is guardian of the secret knowledge of death and resurrection. As Anubis the dog is the attendant of the dead and the soul guide to the land of spirit. The dog is associated with the messenger gods as well as those gods of destruction. The dog, however, has another aspect as well. Dogs are often placed in the company of Mother Goddesses and healers. Dogs, like cats, were regarded as witches' familiars and, as Cooper tells us, "represent witches as rain-makers, hence 'raining cats and dogs.'" [41]

Various age-old tales exist concerning dogs and their supernatural characteristics. A Gypsy belief said that if a dog digs a big hole in your garden, there a death in the family will soon follow. The Radfords

[40] Titcomb, op cit. 59.
[41] Cooper op cit.

offer some anecdotal evidence in support of this belief in the way of some mail that they received:

"About 40 years ago," he wrote," I was told by a gipsy that when a dog digs a big hole in your garden, there will be a death in the family. Last week [February 1945] a dog came in my garden and dug a big hole. I filled it in, but he came again and dug it out. Next day, my brother-in-law's father died. I have not seen the dog since." [42]

To the indigenous people of Japan, the Ainu, dogs were felt to have the ability to detect ghosts. This psychic ability will not be disputed by very many around the world who believe the same thing. Dogs especially among animals seem to have the power to "observe" spirit manifestations.

Dogs have also been linked to healing as well as death. Illnesses were "transferred" to dogs by placing a hair from the ill person between two slices of bread and butter and feeding it to a dog. The dog would catch the cough, measles or whopping cough and the person would recover soon after.

In Holland, the ancient role of dogs in healing has been well documented. In two areas of Holland along the Rhine River, discoveries of ancient altars to the Mother Goddess Nehalennia have been found. One site, uncovered in 1647 on the Isle of Walcheren and the other discovered in 1970 on the East Scheldt Estuary, contain 120 altars, some in depths of over 80 feet. Evidently, these altars are the

---

[42] Radford, Edwin and Mona A. *Encyclopaedia of Superstitions.* New York: The Philosophical Library 1949, 103.

remains of a temple dating back to 200 CE, which sank into the sea. Nehalennia was a domestic goddess that had an impressive following. In fact, both the Romans and Gauls adopted her into their pantheon. Nehalennia invariably appears accompanied with dogs. While mother goddesses do appear with dogs, Nehalennia is pictured with them so often that she is compared to the goddess Epona who is considered a horse-goddess because she is always shown with them. "The symbolism of the dog," according to Miranda Green, "is important here: if we use the mythology of the Graeco-Roman world, the beast could represent either healing or death, both of which are functions of the mothers." [43] Nehalennia is considered a goddess of the sea and protector of fishermen and seamen. This is obvious in that altars that were dedicated at her temple were put there by these sea-going men—given in thanks for her protection. Other gods and goddess often shown with dogs are Diana, Aesculapius (god of healing), Cerberus, Sucellus and Nodens. Nodens actually appears as a dog as his zoomorphic attribute.

Numerous small Mother Goddess figurines have been found in England, Gaul and the Rhineland, which represent fertility and prosperity. According to Davidson, the Goddesses carry fruit, baskets, bunches of grapes, bread and/or eggs. They also have a babe at their breasts or a small dog as a companion. While normally found in threes

[43] Green, Miranda. *The Gods of the Celts.* Gloucester: Alan Sutton 1986, 88.

near rivers, springs or temples, four were found together in London in 1977. [44]

The association with dogs and healing is an ancient one. In Mesopotamia, the sitting dog was used as a divine symbol from the Old Babylonian period through the Neo-Babylonian age (1950 BCE through 539 BCE). Various inscriptions have been found over the years that identify the sitting dog figure "as the symbol of Gula, goddess of healing" [45] and patron of doctors. Several dog figurines have been discovered inside a temple dedicated to Gula in Babylon and another found was dedicated to the Sumerian equivalent of Gula, called Ninisina (known then as "the great doctor of the black-headed," meaning "of the human beings"). Images of the dog were also commonly utilized as protective amulets in Assyria and Babylon. "Groups of five clay figurines of dogs painted different colours were prescribed as foundation deposits for either side of a gateway," report Black and Green. "Bronze dog figurines are in the same period usually found in groups of seven…Whether they were magically protective or dedicatory or served some other purpose is unclear." [46]

Dogs are also considered one of the were-animal species. The Yuman Indians regarded dogs as "people" and would not eat dogs for that reason. In Scotland, it was believed that children were occasionally transformed into white dogs by evil magicians and could only be

---

[44] Davidson, op cit, 109.
[45] Black, Jeremy and Anthony Green. *Gods, Demons and Symbols of Ancient Mesopotamia.* Austin: University of Texas Press 1992, 70.
[46] Ibid.

restored to their human form by striking them with a magic wand or dressing them in shirts made of "bog-cotton." [47]

Black Dogs

Perhaps one of the most intriguing legends associated with dogs is that of the Black Dog. An almost universal tale, the Black Dog is truly a supernatural creature and is associated with sorcery, death and the damned—as well as Hecate. This bit of lore knows no boundaries—being common in Britain and the United States both among indigenous and the dominant Euro-American cultures. Most of the tales speak of a rather nondescript, sometimes large black dog that haunts certain areas—never leaving prints even in the snow. One such story is that of the Black Dog of West Peak, or Black Pond in the hills of central Connecticut. Legend has it that the dog, appearing as a "short-haired, sad-eyed…beast of vague spaniel ancestry" [48] with friendly ways spells doom for any person who sees it three times. The legends say, "if a man shall meet the Black Dog once, it shall be for joy; and if twice, it shall be for sorrow; and the third time, he shall die."[49] Accounts of savage and ghostly Black Dogs have been recorded in England as far back as 1577, often resulting in human fatalities.

Legends of mysterious black dogs also populate the lore of Native Americans. These dogs are some of the many localized supernatural

---

[47] MacKenzie, Donald A. *Ancient Man in Britain.* London: Senate 1996, 190. A reprint of the 1922 edition published by Blackie & Son Ltd, London.
[48] Philips, David E. *Legendary Connecticut: Traditional Tales from the Nutmeg State.* Williamantic: Curbstone Press 1992, 237.
[49] Ibid, 238.

beings, which are always present but normally only seen when tragedy or disaster is imminent. One such account tells of two elderly women who went to a water hole to gather juniper berries, "one of the women saw a big, black dog and thought it a sheepherder's dog. 'It went down the rock into the water below and wasn't seen again'." [50] Like the Black Dog of West Peak, an old Kawaiisu story relates how "old timers saw lots of dog there, but there were no tracks." [51]

Black Dogs have the reputation of being a number of creatures, from simply "dogs" to the ghosts of humans, demons and harbingers of doom. A fifteenth century German manuscript says "the Devil will come in the form of a black dog and will answer all questions." [52]

In addition, while not all of the legends place these apparitions near water, a great many of them are tied to wells, ponds and lakes and the bridges and entryways to these bodies of water. Folklorist Katherine Briggs, referencing Theo Brown's article in the September 1958 issue of *Folk-Lore*, divides reports of Black Dogs into three categories:

1) A shape-shifting demon, called the Barguest,

2) A black dog about calf-size, normally described as shaggy and intensely black; and

---

[50] Zigmond, Maurice L. "The Supernatural World of the Kawaiisu" in Thomas C. Blackburn (ed.) *Flowers of the Wind: Papers on Ritual, Myth, And Symbolism in California and the Southwest*. Socorro: Ballena Press 1977.
[51] Ibid.
[52] Kieckhefer, Richard. *Magic in the Middle Ages.* Cambridge: Cambridge University Press 1989, 162.

3) Black dogs which appear at certain times of the year in a calendar-cycle. [53]

Some stories of Black Dogs regard them as guardian dogs, which reportedly have protected lonely travelers. Researcher Katy Jordan describes these dogs as "usually associated with a particular stretch of road, or a stream, or places of transition like gateways or parish boundaries. They are essentially non-aggressive, kindly and protective beasts, whose role seems to be either to patrol or guard the boundary or road that is their 'beat,' or to protect and guide travellers home." [54]

It is this form of Black Dog that is normally associated with water sites. We may draw a few conclusions as to why they are seen, at least in the British Isles. A pair of dogs was sacrificed at Farnworth in Gloucestershire during the 4th century C.E., two in Southwark dated to the 3rd century and eight pairs in a well in Surrey (along with red-deer antler, two complete dishes and a broken flagon). A recent excavation at an ancient well at Shiptonthorpe in Yorkshire uncovered a number of dog skulls as well as the remains of bundles of mistletoe. Because mistletoe was so important in Druidic rites, this well may have been an important ritual site. A well located near an untouched tomb on Cyprus in the cemetery of the ancient Greek harbor city of Bamboula, has recently yielded a discovery of three-dozen dog

---

[53] Briggs, Katherine. *British Folktales.* New York: Pantheon Books 1977,115.
[54] Jordan, Katy. *The Haunted Landscape: Folklore, ghosts & legends of Wiltshire.* Wiltshire: Ex Libris Press 2000, 174.

skeletons. [55] A pottery shard was also found in the same well with a relief depicting two men and two bulls. The reason for the presence of the dogs is unknown however, the similarities between this Greek well and those found in Britain is striking. If there is a common reason for the dog burials or sacrifices in these wells it would indicate a common tradition or ritual belief dating from, at least, the 13th century BCE through the 3rd century CE.

It is believed that one reason for sacrificing dogs was to provide eternal "guardians of place."[56] The fact that many are seen near gateways and bridges would indicate that these animals are, as spirit helpers, fulfilling that intent. These explanations do not address those mysterious Black Dogs seen in the United States, however guardian dogs are common in shamanic lore all over the world as guardians and guides to the Otherworld.

Bob Trubshaw wrote, "few myths have such world-wide parallels. We are left with the distinct impression that dogs have been protecting the ways to the Otherworld back into the origins of human beliefs." [57]

Other animals are also associated with wells, water sources, and the connection between the world of the living and the Otherworld where the dead and other creatures of mystery reside. White cattle, stags and hounds are some of those denizens of the Underworld. Like the Black

---

[55] Anon. "Intact Tomb from Bronze Age Cyprus" in Archaeology Odyssey, May/June 2003, Vol 6 No. 3, 21.
[56] Another purpose recorded in Japan was to sacrifice a black dog to obtain rain.
[57] Trubshaw, Bob. "Black Dogs: Guardians of the corpse ways" in At The Edge, August 2001 http://www.indigogroup.co.uk/edge/bdogs.htm.

Dogs, the Kawaiisu also have stories about white dogs, which frequent sacred waters. Zigmond wrote about one such occurrence:

"Near Paiute Ranch there is a spring where the water used to come out of the ground like a fountain. There were lots of reeds growing there and so it was called 'by the reed-water'. A white dog lived there. Old timers saw him lying off to one side. 'Maybe he lived in the water.'"[58]

Dogs played an important role in Meso-American lore as guides for the souls of the dead to the Underworld. Alexander wrote, in his somewhat "Noble Savage" account of the journey of the soul to its final resting place, "…the perils of the Underworld Way were to be passed, and the soul to arrive before Mictlantecutli, whence after four years he should fare onward until, by the aid of his dog, sacrificed at his grave, he should pass over the Ninefold Stream, and thence, hound with master, enter into the eternal house of the dead…"[59]

W.Y. Evans-Wentz interviewed an Irish man from Galway during the early years of 1900 that spoke of a "fairy dog":

"…Steven pointed to a rocky knoll in a field not far from his home, and said:--'I saw a dog with a white ring around his neck by that hill there, and the oldest men round Galway have seen him too, for he

---

[58] Zigmond, op cit. 1977.

[59] Alexander, Hartley Burr. *The World's Rim: Great Mysteries of the North American Indians.* New York: Dover Publications Inc. 1999, 201-202.

has been here for one hundred years or more. He is a dog of the *good people*, and only appears at certain times of the night." [60]

On the Isle of Man, the Fairy Dog was called the Moddey Doo (also known as the "Mauthe Doog")—Manx for "Black Dog." However, it has also been described as "white as driven snow." [61]

Tales of fairy dogs seem to contradict other stories of dogs being the enemy of fairies, mermaids and demons, "especially cave-haunting demons." [62] "In the folk-stories of Scotland," wrote MacKenzie, "dogs help human beings to attack and overcome supernatural beings." [63]

However, the Fairy did in fact, have their pet dogs too. Called *cu sith* which means "fairy dog" they acted as guides to the fairy land and to the Underworld. They can be differentiated from "normal" dogs by their color, normally green or white with red ears. Fairy dogs were commonly believed to be a dark green in color with the ears being a darker green and the legs running a lighter green color. Its long tail, according to Campbell, was "rolled up in a coil on its back, but others have the tail flat and plaited like the straw rug of a pack-saddle." [64] The famous fairy dog of Fin mac Coul, however, had yellow feet, black sides, white belly, green back and two pointed blood-red ears. In Wales, pure white dogs are thought to be fairy dogs.

---

[60] Evans-Wentz, W.Y. *The Fairy-Faith in Celtic Countries.* Mineola: Dover Publications Inc. 2002, 40.
[61] Ibid, 120.
[62] MacKenzie, op cit., 65.
[63] Ibid, 66.
[64] Campbell, John Gregorson. *The Gaelic Otherworld*, edited by Ronald Black. Edinburgh: Birlinn Ltd., 200516.

According to Anna Franklin, "The fairy dog makes its lair in the clefts of rocks and travels in a straight line. It barks only three times and by the time the third bark is heard the victim is overtaken, unless he has reached a place of safety." [65]

Ghost Dogs

Black dogs are, of course, ghost dogs. However, there are very many stories concerning even more mysterious and ghostly apparitions of canines. One such encounter occurred in Pemiscot county Missouri—deep in the Ozarks. According to folklorist Vance Randolph, "Some night hunters…swore they saw an enormous black dog, fully eight feet long, without any head. They came close to the creature, and one man threw his ax at it, but the ax passed right through the body of the booger dog and stuck fast in a tree." [66] Another headless dog was frequently seen near Braggadocio, Missouri running through the town on moonlit nights. "It behaves just like any other dog, but it is clearly headless," wrote Randolph. [67]

"Black Dogs," wrote Jennifer Westwood in her book *Albion*, "were in some places thought to be the ghosts of the unquiet dead. The wicked Lady Howard in Devon was so transformed…" [68]

---

[65] Franklin, Anna. *The Illustrated Encyclopaedia of Fairies.* London: Paper Tiger 2004, 68.

[66] Randolph, Vance.*Ozark Magic and Folklore.* New York: Dover Publications, Inc. 1964, 224. A reprint of *Ozark Superstitions* published by Columbia University Press 1947.

[67] Ibid, 225.

[68] Westwood, Jennifer. *Albion: A Guide to Legendary Britain.* London: Paladin/Grafton Books 1985, 176.

And of course, we cannot fail to mention the hounds of the Wild Huntsman. Various locations around England and Europe in general, claim the Huntsman. Referred to in some locals as the "Wish Hounds" ("Wish" being a local word for the Devil)[69] these ferocious dogs with glowing red eyes accompany the Lord of Death on his swift horse—hunting for the souls of men. "Throughout all Aryan mythology," noted John Fiske, "the souls of the dead are supposed to ride on the night-wind, with their howling dogs, gathering into their throng the souls of those just dying as they pass by their houses." [70] Dogs that would sit under the window of seriously ill persons were thought to portend the coming death and it was customary in 19th century Europe to open the windows in homes after the death of a person "in order that the soul may not be hindered in joining the mystic cavalcade." [71]

Dog-Men

Various legends about dog-men have been related generation after generation in various locations around the world. In pre-revolutionary China there were of four clans of people called the Jung who worshipped the dog because, to them, the dog was their ancestor. According to legend, a dog requested the hand of a Chinese princess but was refused by her father unless the dog was able to change into the form of a man. This he almost did, his body was that of a man but his head remained that of a dog. Until the early 1920's the Jung wore a

---

[69] Other names for these Black Dogs are Gabriel Hounds, Dando or Dandy Dogs, and in Wales the Cwm Annwn, the Hounds of Hell.
[70] Fiske, op cit 76.
[71] Ibid.

large headpiece that entirely covered the head, the explanation being that they still had dog features due to their dog ancestor. [72]

Similar tales of the mating between human females and male wolves or dogs, resulting in a race of dog-men, are frequently found in Native American mythology. A race of dog-men also appears in Hawaiian mythology. "Among the peoples said to have appeared during the fifth period of the Kumulipo,"[73] wrote Martha Beckwith, "are the dog people…They lived in the sand hills [on Maui and Kauai] and they had mystical power of the demigods…in the form of big war dogs. These dog people still appear on Maui in the procession of spirits known as 'Marchers of the night.' They look like other human beings but have tails like a dog." [74] These "dog people" were a well known class of Hawaiians said to have hairless bodies and well versed in wrestling and "bone breaking." Some were considered professional robbers and others as cannibals. Other dog-men are described as dogs with human bodies and having supernatural power who used to terrorize the countryside.

Various myths and legends of Dog-Men exist in Hawaiian tradition. "The Great Dog Ku" is one of these. Ku, the Dog Man, was a spirit being that, one day "decided to come down from the clouds

---

[72] Werner, E.T.C. *Myths and Legends of China.* New York: Dover Publications, Inc. 1994, 419-423.

[73] The "Kumulipo" is a chant of 2,077 lines, which tells of the creation of the world and the genealogy of a young Chief by the name of Keawe who lived in the 1700s.

[74] Beckwith, Martha. *Hawaiian Mythology.* Honolulu: University of Hawaii Press 1970, 343.

and visit mankind." [75] Ku was able to change at will from his dog form to that of a man. Unfortunately, Ku desired the daughter of the High Chief who refused Ku's advances. A savage war ensued with Ku striking as lightning and he killed and devoured many of the Hawaiian people. Eventually many men fought Ku and killed him with spears and clubs. They cut Ku's body into two pieces which were thrown far apart and turned to stone by the priests. These stones were reportedly venerated for many years by the Hawaiian people.

In many legends, it is this race of human-like dogs and wolves that are the creators of humankind. Some dog-men, such as the Egyptian jackal-headed Anubis became gods in their own right. Or, in the Christian sense, they became saints.

There are two types of dog-men. One, cynanthropy are the Dog-men that, according to David Gordon White, are "a hybrid creature who, while more human than the domesticated dog, is nonhuman in the sense that he belongs to an 'other' or foreign race, yet human in his social behavior." [76] The second form is the Cynocephalic—human in form except it has a dog, wolf or jackal head, such as Anubis.

Monstrous races of beings were commonly believed in during the early years of the Christian church. Irish legend, according to

---

[75] Westervelt, William D. *Myths and Legends of Hawaii.* Honolulu: Mutual Publishing 1987, 202

[76] White, David Gordon. *Myths of the Dog-Man.* Chicago: University of Chicago Press 1991, 16.

MacCulloch, "speaks of men with cat, dog, or goat heads." [77] As with any other Pagan symbol, or place or deity they became important to the Christian theology as well. St. Augustine in his writings "saved" these creatures and, as White states, they "eventually became Christendom's favorite foils in the lives of the missionary saints who pacified, converted, domesticated, and placed them in the service of the Catholic cause." [78]

One of these dog-headed beings, Christopher, became a Catholic saint, at least in Gnostic and Coptic texts. According to White, "Christopher's Christian hagiography may be summarized as follows: He is a giant belonging to a cynocephalic race, in the land of the Channeans (the 'Canines' of the New Testament), who eat human flesh and whose only form of communication is barking (*latrare*). His original name, Réprebos…'the Condemned' corresponds to his nature: he is black, pagan, ferocious, and dreadful." [79]

According to the Coptic text, he is persuaded by Christ to fight against the Pagan armies until St. Babylus at Antioch baptize him. At this time, his skin becomes "white as milk" and he looses his canine characteristics. Christopher was depicted with a dogs head until the beginning of the 19th century on Eastern churches, bridges, city gates etc. Most of these images were destroyed by the iconoclasts at that

---

[77] MacCulloch, J.A. *The Religion of the Ancient Celts.* Mineola: Dover Publications, Inc.2003, 217.
[78] Ibid, 19.
[79] Ibid, 34.

time and are rare to be found except on a few illuminated manuscript pages.

The statues and carvings of Anubis in Egypt, as well as carvings dating back to 6600 BCE in the Sahara desert of a dog-headed man, are evidence of an ancient belief in dog-headed humanoids. According to French art-historian Jean-Pierre Mohen more than 140 dog-headed figures found so far "express the imaginary and symbolic relationships between man and animal rather than any hunting techniques." [80] The carvings show creatures with "superhuman" strength and, write Mohen, "they exist to carry out sacred tasks." [81] Do these images represent the nature of the dog as the guardian of the secrets of death and rebirth? Alternatively, do they represent creatures divine in their own right?

The Serpent, Toad and Frog

The serpent was highly sacred to Hecate. The serpent is a creature representative of death and rebirth as is Hecate. Like other snake-goddesses, Hecate is guardian of women and childbirth.

Frogs have been connected with witches because they were associated with Hecate—the goddess of witches. Frogs were also sacred to the Roman goddess Venus, who is another aspect of Hecate. Heket, the Egyptian Hecate, was a frog goddess "who assisted in

---

[80] Mohen, Jean-Pierre. *Prehistoric Art: The Mythical Birth of Humanity.* Paris: Pierre Terrail/Telleri 2002, 185.
[81] Ibid, 184.

fashioning the child in the womb and who presided over its birth." [82] As a sacred midwife, Hecate was depicted in Egyptian art as a frog or as a woman with a frog's head. Amulets of the goddess were simply in the image of frogs but were inscribed, "I am the Resurrection." [83] Heket's image often appeared on wands made of ivory during the Middle Kingdom. Such wands, called Apotropaic, were usually made of hippopotamus ivory but could also be constructed of calcite, ebony or faience. According to Oakes and Gahlin, "All manner of weird and wonderful magical imagery decorate these wands, including dancing baboons, snake-breathing lions, winged quadrupeds, human-headed winged snakes," and other fantastical images. [84]

Any inscriptions made on these wands were protective in manner and normally refer to the well-being of women and children.

Babylonian cylinder seals depicted nine frogs as a fertility charm, the frogs representing the Ninefold Goddess that ruled the nine months of gestation.

As Hecate's amulets indicated that she is synonymous with resurrection, so too is the frog which represents her. The frog also came to be regarded as the protector of mothers and newborn children in Egyptian society, and represented fertility, new life, abundance and

---

[82] Wilkinson, Richard H. *The Complete Gods and Goddesses of Ancient Egypt.* Lonson: Thames and Hudson Ltd. 2003, 229.
[83] Budge, Sir E.A. Wallis. *Egyptian Magic.* New York: Dover Publications Inc. 1971, 63.
[84] Oakes, Lorna and Lucia Gahlin. *Ancient Egypt.* New York: Barnes & Noble, Inc. 2006, 453.

the embryonic powers of water. The frog's association with fertility was also accepted in the Greco-Roman world.

"The snake is a main image of the vitality and continuity of life," wrote anthropologist Marija Gimbutas, "the guarantor of life energy in the home, and the symbol of family and animal life." [85] The snake means something different and yet the same in many cultures and locations. The serpent is a feared goddess of the river, a messenger and spirit being of Native America, a water spirit and god of Africa. These are similar characteristics for a universally important symbol. There is an opposite view, however. The snake is also portrayed as Satan himself in Biblical lore. As historian Jean Markale wrote, "Western religious thought has been almost unanimous in making the serpent of Genesis into a concrete representation of the tempter, that is to say, of Satan himself, relying for support upon the Apocalypse where this 'great serpent'…is the image of absolute evil." [86] The serpent had been respected as a symbol of wisdom and life renewed for thousands of years—until the Hebrews and then the Christians waged successful campaigns to destroy it. "When the Hebrews introduced a male god into Canaan," says Mark O'Connell and Raje Airey, "the female deity and the snake were relegated and associated with evil." [87] Later, the Christian campaign was able to, as Page Bryant wrote, "distort a

---

[85] Gimbutas, Marija. *The Civilization of the Goddess: The World of Old Europe.* San Francisco: HarperSanFrancisco 1991, 236.
[86] Markale, Jean. *The Great Goddess: Reverence of the Devine Feminine From the Paleolithic to the Present.* Rochester: Inner Traditions 1999, 6.
[87] O'Connell, Mark and Raje Airey. *The Complete Encyclopedia of Signs & Symbols.* London: Hermes House 2005, 186.

positive and ancient pagan symbol to suit the purposes of Christianity."[88]

Even before Christianity established a toehold however, the serpent was viewed by the Hebrews as either possessed by Satan or was Satan himself. In Jewish folklore, the original serpent walked on two legs, talked and ate the same food that Adam and Eve did. One day the serpent witnessed Adam and Eve engaged in sexual relations, and he became jealous—persuading Eve to eat the forbidden fruit. In punishment, according to Hebrew legend, "its hands and legs were cut off, so it had to crawl on its belly, all food it ate tasted of dust, and it became the eternal enemy of man."[89] However, the serpent also was able to have sexual relations with Eve before he was punished by God. Because of this the Israelites only became purified when they stood at Mt. Sinai and received the torah. "Gentiles, however," according to Alan Untermann, "have never been cleansed of this serpentine impurity."[90]

Christian hatred of the serpent was not universal however. In Armenian folklore, according to Anthony S. Mercatante, "Christ himself is identified with Shahapet, a beneficient serpent spirit who inhabited olive trees and vinestocks in the ancient mythology."[91]

---

[88] Bryant, Page. *Awakening Arthur!* London: The Aquarian Press 1991, 64

[89] Unterman, Alan. *Dictionary of Jewish Lore & Legend.* New York: Thames and Hudson 1991, 176.

[90] Ibid.

[91] Mercatante, Anthony S. *Good and Evil in Myth & Legend.* New York: Barnes & Noble 1978, 65.

A graven image of a serpent suspended from a cross-like beam was erected by Moses to protect the Hebrews from the poisonous bite of serpents. Acting on God's instructions, "...Moses made a serpent of brass, and put it upon a pole, and it came to pass, that if a serpent had bitten any man, when he beheld the serpent of brass, he lived." [92]

Sinners transformed into snake creatures in Hell

On the base of one of the ancient menhirs in Carnac an image of five snakes standing on their tails was carved. "When the site was excavated," writes archaeologist Johannes Maringer, "in 1922, five axes were found under the engravings. The blades faced upward; obviously the axes had been deliberately placed in that position. It is most likely

[92] Numbers 21:9, KJV

that even in Neolithic times the serpent was a symbol of life." [93] Maringer believes that the serpent was closely associated with deceased ancestors and the five serpents engraved on the menhir probably indicated that five people were buried there along with the axes.

The duality of meanings most likely originated in the contrasting views of the serpent in Old European and Indo-European mythology. In Old European lore (prior to 4500 BCE) the serpent was benevolent, a symbol of life and fertility in both plants and animals (including humans), protective of the family and of domestic livestock. "Snakes are guardians of the springs of life and immortality," wrote Spanish scholar J.E. Cirlot, "and also of those superior riches of the spirit that are symbolized by hidden treasure." [94] The poisonous snake in Old European lore was, according to Gimbutas, "an epiphany of the Goddess of Death." [95] Indo-European mythology (evolving between 4000 and 2500 BCE) contrasted this view, regarding the snake as a symbol of evil, an epiphany of the God of Death, and an adversary of the Thunder God. This was the point in time that the Goddess religion began to give way to that of the male dominated religion of the Sky God.

Gimbutas goes on to say, "it is not the body of the snake that was sacred, but the energy exuded by this spiraling or coiling creature

---

[93] Maringer, Johannes. *The Gods of Prehistoric Man: History of Religion.* London: Phoenix Press 2002, 170-171.

[94] Cirlot. J. E. *A Dictionary of Symbols, 2nd Edition.* New York: Barnes & Noble Books 1995, 286.

[95] Gimbutas, op cit, 400.

which transcends its boundaries and influences the surrounding world."[96]

In the Classic world the serpent was the creator of the universe, it laid the Cosmic Egg and split it asunder to form the heavens and the earth. As Hans Leisgang wrote, "This serpent, which coiled round the heavens, biting its tail, was the cause of solar and lunar eclipses. In the Hellenistic cosmology, this serpent is assigned to the ninth, starless spheres of the planets and the zodiac. This sphere goes round the heavens and the earth and also under the earth, and governs the winds."[97] "In Christian theology," Leisegang continues, "this serpent became the prince of the world, the adversary of the transcendental God, the dragon of the outer darkness, who has barred off this world from above, so that it can be redeemed only by being annihilated."[98]

This creator-serpent, the Great Serpent, was symbolic of the sun, not evil but "the good spirit of light" as Leisegang so aptly describes it. It is this Great Serpent that is cause and ruler of the four seasons, the four winds and the four quarters of the cosmos.

A white snake, like the salmon, was a source for wisdom and magical power and was associated with the goddess/Saint Brigit, also known in England and Scotland as Bride. On February 1st, Bride's Day

---

[96] Gimbutas, Marija. *The Language of the Goddess*. San Francisco: HarperSanFrancisco 1991, 121.
[97] Leisegang, Hans. "The Mystery of the Serpent" in *Pagan and Christian Mysteries: Papers from the Eranos Yearbook*, edited by Joseph Campbell. New York: The Bollingen Foundation/Harper & Row Publishers 1955, 26-27.
[98] Ibid, 27.

the serpent woke for its winter hibernation to bring in the change in seasons from winter to spring. Mackenzie relates an old Gaelic charm:

> "To-day is the day of Bride,
> The serpent shall come from his hole;
> I will not molest the serpent
> And the serpent will not molest me."[99]

The many serpent-like symbols found in ancient rock art the world over testify to the importance of this animal in the human mind. The zigzag and meandering lines symbolic of water, the mysterious spirals found the world over which mimic the coiled serpent all speak of the underlying mystery that humans have felt towards the snake and the snakes place in the mythos of the Otherworld and death. However, not only death, for many the snake represented life and the renewal of life. The snake was the feared guardian of life and the forces of life as well as the messenger to and from the world of the dead. Snakes were believed to be symbolic of the departed soul to the ancient Greeks. It was also valued as a guardian of temples, treasuries and oracles, its eyesight believed to be especially keen to allow it to effectively guard against intrusion. Joseph Campbell noted that "in India…the 'serpent

---

[99] Mackenzie, Donald A. *Ancient Man in Britain.* London: Senate 1996, 188-189. A reprint of the 1922 edition published by Blackie & Son Limited, London.

kings' guard both the waters of immortality and the treasures of the earth."[100]

While many male anthropologist and archaeologist argue that the serpent is symbolic of fertility (as a phallic symbol), art historian Merlin Stone offers another view:

"[The serpent] appears to have been primarily revered as a female in the Near and Middle East and generally linked to wisdom and prophetic counsel rather than fertility and growth as is so often suggested."[101]

This statement is not entirely true. The god Ningišzida ("Lord of the Good Tree") was an important male deity in Mesopotamia. As an underworld god, he was guardian over demons and at least one Sumerian ruler regarded Ningišzida as his personal protector. While primarily a god of the underworld there is one myth ("Adapa at the gate of heaven") that has Ningišzida as one of the guardians at the gates of heaven. [102] "The symbol and beast of Ningišzida," according to Black and Green, "was the horned snake…" [103]

The snake and the serpent have been depicted as goddesses and gods, as holy beings to be worshipped, as dragons, as devils and as symbols of lust, greed and sin—and of death. In mythic lore, Zeus

---

[100] Campbell, Joseph. *Creative Mythology: The Masks of God Volume IV.* London: Secker & Warburg 1968, 120.
[101] Stone, Merlin. *When God Was A Woman.* New York: Barnes & Noble Books 1993, 199.
[102] Black, Jeremy and Anthony Green. *Gods, Demons and Symbols of Ancient Mesopotamia.* Austin: University of Texas Press 2000, 139.
[103] Ibid 140.

appears in snake form to mate with Persephone who thereafter gives birth to Dionysos, "the god who in Crete, it so happens, was synonymous with Zeus." [104] The serpent is "the emblem of all self-creative divinities and represents the generative power of the earth. It is solar, chthonic, sexual, funerary and the manifestation of force at any level, a source of all potentialities both material and spiritual," writes J.C. Cooper, "and closely associated with the concepts of both life and death." [105]

The Giants of classic Greek and Roman mythology reportedly had snake-like legs as did the founder of Athens, Cecrops. Cecrops, a semi-serpent, was considered an innovator of his day, abolishing blood sacrifice, introducing basic laws of marriage, politics and property and encouraging the worship of Zeus and Athena. [106] Again, a duality exists between these two creatures with snake-like characteristics. The Giants were enemies of Zeus and were defeated by Hercules on behalf of the gods of Olympus and Cecrops was a champion for the causes of Zeus.

Recent excavations in the Kenar Sandal area in Jiroft, Iran have uncovered additional serpent-legged figures. According to the *Persian Journal*,[107] the relief's depicting two men with "snake tails instead of

---

[104] Baring, Anne and Jules Cashford. *The Myth of the Goddess: Evolution of an Image.* London: Arkana/Penguin Books 1991, 317.
[105] Cooper, J.C. *An Illustrated Encyclopaedia of Traditional Symbols.* London : Thames and Hudson 1978, 147.
[106] Cotterell, Arthur. *The Encyclopedia of Mythology: Classical, Celtic, Greek.* London: Hermes House 2005, 84.
[107] "New Stone Reliefs Discovered in Jiroft, Iran" in *Persian Journal*, February 2, 2006. http://www.iranian.ws/iran_news/publish/article_12873.shtml

legs" were carved on soapstone on a "flat stone cliff." At one time almost 5,000 years ago, Kenar Sandal was an important trade city for the Persian Gulf region, linking what is now present day Afghanistan, Pakistan, Iran and Tajikistan. The relief's of serpent-men indicate that this image has an ancient origin most likely outside the classic Greco-Roman world.

Zeus conquers the Serpent-legged Titans

In support of the view that this mythic creature originated in the non-Classic World are the serpent-men of the Indian Underworld, the "demonic Cobras" called the Nagas. According to Mackenzie "they are of human form to the waist, the rest of their bodies being like those of serpents." [108] The Nagas were demi-gods to the Indian serpent worshippers and were, according to Mackenzie, "occasionally 'the

---

[108] Mackenzie, Donald A. *India Myths & Legends.* London: Studio Editions 1993, 65.

friends of man', and to those they favoured they gave draughts of their nectar, which endowed them with great strength."[109]

Abrasax Gem Amulet

An interesting image similar to the serpent-legged Titans and the Nagas is that carved upon the strange "Abrasax gems", magical amulets introduced in the second century that mingled early Christian and Pagan themes. Originating in Alexandria, the images most certainly were inspired by the mystic powers of the man-serpent as represented by the Titans.

It is interesting to note that Athens has even more connections to serpent-men in the form of Erichthonius—the first king of Athens. According to legend, this serpent being was created from the semen of the smith-god Hephaistos. Hephaistos had attempted to rape Athena but she miraculously disappeared just in time. His semen, as it fell to

[109] Ibid., 66.

the earth, grew into the serpent Erichthonius. Ely offers an alternative view: "In the days of Pausanias, Hephaistos and Gaia were said to be the parents of Erichthonius." This version evidently arose from the more conservative elements of Greek society that could not abide with the original creation of the serpent-being from an act of rape. [110]

In Mesoamerican traditions, the Plumed Serpent, Quetzalcoatl, called "the wise instructor," brings culture and knowledge to the people and "takes charge or interferes in creative activities" of the world. [111] It is Quetzalcoatl who discovers corn and provides it for humankind's nourishment. While historical lore indicates that Quetzalcoatl was a man (in fact, a tall, white man with a beard), he is symbolically represented as a serpent on many temple complexes, the most notable being at Chichen-Itza in Yucatan. During certain times of the year the steps the lead up the pyramid temple cast an undulating shadow that connects with the carved stone serpent heads—bringing to life the Plumed Serpent.

The serpent also represents chaos, corruption and darkness along with knowledge and spirit. It is this knowledge that the Bible uses to evict Adam and Eve from paradise and what brings the snake so much hatred. It is the symbolism of the snake, that is so closely associated with the Earth and the Earth's creative powers that the followers of

---

[110] Ely, Talfourd. *The Gods of Greece and Rome.* Mineola: Dover Publications Inc. 2003, 161. A reprint of the 1891 edition published by G.P. Putnam's Sons, New York.

[111] Bierhorst, John. *The Mythology of Mexico and Central America.* New York: William Morrow and Company 1990, 145.

the Sky God wished to destroy. According to Andrews, the snake "threatened the world order established by the sky gods and continually tried to return the world to its original state of chaos."[112]

The serpent, in fact, threatened the order and control of the Judeo-Christian religion. As Markale suggests, Eve disobeyed the patriarchal priests and listens to the serpent, the serpent being representative of the Mother Goddess. "This is a case, pure and simple, of a return to the mother-goddess cult, a true 'apostasy' as it were, and thus a very grave sin against the patriarchal type of religion that Yahweh represents."[113] Markale and others, most notably the French Catholic priest André de Smet, believe that the original sin was the first battle in the long struggle between the patriarchal religion of Yahweh and the matriarchal religion of the Mother Goddess. The "curse against the serpent," Markale writes, "…is against the mother goddess herself." [114]

The Gnostic writers viewed the serpent in a different manner. The Kabbalist Joseph Gikatila wrote in his book *Mystery of the Serpent*:

"Know and believe that the Serpent, at the beginning of creation, was indispensable to the order of the world, so long as he kept his place; and he was a great servant…and he was needed for the ordering of all the chariots, each in its place…It is he who moves the spheres and turns them from East to the West and from North to the South.

---

[112] Andrews, Tamra. *A Dictionary of Nature Myths.* Oxford: Oxford University Press 1998, 176.
[113] Markale, op cit, 6.
[114] Ibid, 7.

Without him there would have been neither seed nor germination, nor will to produce any created thing."[115]

The Ophites, a successor group of the original Gnostics, venerated the snake. To the Ophites the serpent was made by God to be "the cause of Gnosis for mankind…It was the serpent…who taught man and woman the complete knowledge of the mysteries on high" which resulted in the serpent being "cast down from the heavens." [116] To this group the snake was the "living symbol of the celestial image that they worshipped."[117] According to Doresse, the Ophites kept and fed serpents in special baskets and met near the serpent's burrows. They would arrange loaves of bread on a table and then lure the snakes to the "offering." The Ophite followers would not partake of the bread however until "each on kissing the muzzle of the reptile they had charmed. This, they claimed, was the perfect sacrifice, the true Eucharist."[118] To the Gnostic Christians, serpent worship was associated with the "restoration of Paradise, and release thereby from the bondages of time." [119]

A similar ritual has taken place each August 15th on the Greek island of Kefalonia. On this day, also known as the feast of the Falling Asleep of the Virgin, in the small village of Markopoulo, small snakes with a small cross-like mark on their heads slither through a

---

[115] As quoted by Jean Doresse, *The Secret Books of the Egyptian Gnostics*. New York: MJF Books 1986, 292-293.
[116] Ibid, 44.
[117] Ibid, 45.
[118] Ibid, 44.
[119] Campbell, op cit. 151.

churchyard, emerging near the bell tower and make their way toward the church. According to witnesses, the snakes enter the church building through bell rope holes in the wall; crawl over the furniture and even over the worshippers as they sit in the pews. The snakes continue onward to the bishop's throne and, as a group, to the icon of the Virgin.

After the service, the serpents disappear and not seen again until the same evening a year later. The people of Markopoulo look forward to the appearance of these creatures as a sign of good luck and bountiful harvests. Only two years in recent memory did not see the return of the snakes. One was in 1940. The next year Greece was invaded by the Axis Forces. The year following their non-appearance in 1953 saw the area devastated by a catastrophic earthquake.

Normally avoiding human contact during their visits to the church the snakes appear quite tame and allow the residents to handle them at will. According to local lore, the annual serpent appearance dates to 1705 when Barbarossa pirates attacked the village. The nuns who resided in the village convent prayed to the Virgin to transform them into snakes to avoid being captured by the pirates, or worse. When the pirates finally gained access to the convent, they were shocked to see the floors, walls and icons writhing with snakes. The snakes have returned each year except for the two previously mentioned.

The serpent, as a representative of the mother goddess, is known from the serpent priestesses of Crete and various other mother goddess locations from the Neolithic. The shrine at Gournia, Crete yielded three figures of the mother goddess. One that shows the mother goddess with a serpent curled around her waist and over one shoulder.[120] The Greek mother goddess Ge or Gaia is often associated with the "earth snake."

Twenty-one figurines of serpent goddesses have been found at Poduri, Romania dating to 4800-4600 BCE indicating that this goddess was not only an ancient one but commonly worshiped throughout Europe and the Middle East. Archaeologist Marija Gimbutas wrote "Their lack of arms, their snake-shaped heads, and the snakes coiling over their abdomens suggest that they represent the Snake Goddess and her attendants, only one of them has an arm raised to her face, a gesture of power." [121]

"Undulating serpents or dragons signify cosmic rhythm, or the power of the waters." [122] The serpent has been associated with water since time began. They appear in Native American rock art throughout the continent symbolic of messengers of the otherworld that traverse through streams, rivers and time through the cracks in stone. It is by no accident that the Plumed Serpent of Mesoamerica is closely associated with the Cosmic Waters or that the Serpent Mound in the Ohio Valley is located near a flowing river. It is also not an accident that accounts of sea serpents are rampant in the world's maritime lore.

---

[120] Mackenzie, Donald A. *Myths and Legends Crete & Pre-Hellenic.* London: Senate 1995, 261. A reprint of the 1917 edition published as *Crete & Pre-Hellenic Europe* by The Gresham Publishing Company, London.
[121] Gimbutas, op cit, 343.
[122] Cooper, op cit, 148.

In the Southwest, snakes were pecked or painted onto rock surfaces designating good or bad water sources. The snake was believed by Native Americans, as well as to the people of Old Europe and the ancient Near East, to bring rain when it is needed. Both the Hopi and Shasta Indians carried live snakes in their mouths for ritual dances used in rainmaking ceremonies[123] and the Cheyenne also danced with poisonous snakes in their "crazy dances." "Crazy dances" were performed to aid in the cure of a sick child, to ensure victory in war or to obtain other blessings for the tribe.[124]

Snakes have also contributed to weather folklore around the world associated with rain. Nineteenth century folklorist Richard Inwards noted, "the chief characteristic of the serpents throughout the East in all ages seems to have been their power over the wind and rain, which they gave or withheld, according to their good or ill will towards man."[125] It was also possible to induce rain, according to Inwards, by hanging a dead snake on a tree. [126]

Mesoamerican traditions "have been recorded," writes anthropologist Robert Rands, "which directly connect the serpent with surface water, rain, and lightning. …a few stray facts regarding the relationship of snakes to the anthropomorphic rain deities of the Maya and Mexicans may be noted. In the Maya codices, the serpent…and

---

[123] Kasner, Leone Letson. *Spirit Symbols in Native American Art.* Philomath: Ayers Mountain Press 1992, 113.
[124] Mooney, James. *The Ghost-Dance Religion and the Sioux Outbreak of 1890.* Chicago: The University of Chicago Press 1965, 273.
[125] Inwards, Richard. *Weather Lore.* London: Elliot Stock 1893.
[126] Ibid.

water are frequently shown together...As giant celestial snakes or as partly anthropomorphized serpents, the Chicchans are rain and thunder deities of the present-day Chorti. ...In modern Zoque belief, snakes serve as the whips of the thunderbolts." [127]

The snake with its fluid motions is a natural symbol of flowing water. Native Americans and others saw this symbolism in the meandering streams and rivers that flow through their lands. They also saw the annual shedding of its skin as a renewal of life and of fertility, a renewal of the fertility that water also provides.

"The serpent is the foundation of the universe," writes Indian artist Jyoti Sahi. "Coiled around the naval of the cosmos, it appears to be the dynamic centre of time and space. The serpent seems always to be moving and yet always still, like the oceans whose waves seem in perpetual turmoil and unrest, but whose boundaries remain fixed, and whose depths are eternal." [128]

In ancient Indian mythology, the serpent becomes the victim of mankind, "...in order to overcome the wilderness...and make it orderly and cultivated...[man] had to injure the serpent..." [129] Sahi says that this injury to the serpent is a "sin" and that the story really "represents the overthrowing of pre-Aryan serpent worship." [130]

---

[127] Rands, Robert L. "Some Manifestations of Water in Mesoamerican Art," Anthropological Papers, No. 48, Bureau of American Ethnology Bulletin 157. Washington: Smithsonian Institution 1955, 361, pgs 265-393.

[128] Sahi, Jyoti. *The Child and the Serpent: Reflections on Popular Indian Symbols.* London: Arkana/Penguin Books 1980, 161.

[129] Ibid, 165.

[130] Ibid, 166.

In the ancient Mesopotamian city of Ur, the snake god Irhan was worshipped. To these people Irhan was representative of the Euphrates River. The mildly poisonous horned vipers of the Middle East gradually assumed the dragon form that we still recognize today.

A snake-dragon called *mušhuššu*, or "furious snake" was worshipped in Babylon at least during the reign of Nebuchadnezzar II (604-562 BCE). This creature with the body and neck of a serpent, lion's forelegs and a bird's hindlegs, was originally an attendant of the city god Ninazu of Ešnunna. The snake-dragon was transferred as an attendant of Ninazu to several other national gods through the years, surviving as a protective pendant through the Hellenistic Period. [131]

Mithras and his salvation-seeking serpent

[131] Jeremy and Anthony Green. *Gods, Demons and Symbols of Ancient Mesopotamia.* Austin: University of Texas Press 2000, 166.

The serpent was present in the liturgy and symbolism of the Mithraic religion as well. Mithraism almost dominated Christianity during the 2nd and 3rd centuries and many Christian symbols are derived from this ancient religion. The snake appears often in paintings and carvings of Mithras hunting, the serpent is present as a companion to the god. Some depict the serpent seeking the flowing sacrificial blood of the bull that was slain in Mithraic baptisms. This, according to writer D. Jason Cooper, "seems to indicate the snake is seeking salvation."[132]

Snakes are also associated with healing. The caduceus, the staff with two intertwined serpents, is found not only in the healing temples of Greece, but also in Native American, Mesoamerican and Hindu symbolism. The snake with its annual shedding of its skin was a logical symbol for life, renewal and protection. In Celtic lands as well the snake was, like the sacred well, associated with healing. To the Sumerians the caduceus was the symbol of life. The caduceus was also an important symbol to some Gnostic Christians who, according to Barbara Walker, "worshipped the serpent hung on a cross…or Tree of Life, calling it Christ the Savior, also a title of Hermes the Wise Serpent represented by his own holy caduceus…" [133] According to Wallis Budge, "the symbol of [the Bablyonian god of healing, Ningishzida] was a staff round which a double-sexed, two-headed serpent called

[132] Cooper, D. Jason. *Mithras: Mysteries and Initiation Rediscovered.* York Beach: Samuel Weiser, Inc. 1996, 74.
[133] Walker, Barbara G. *The Women's Encyclopedia of Myths and Secrets.* Edison: Castle Books 1996, 131.

Sachan was coiled, and a form of this is the recognized mark of the craft of the physician at the present day." [134] The Greek god of healing, Aesculapius was also depicted in a statue at Epidaurus "holding a staff in one hand, while his other hand rested on the head of a snake…"[135]

In Africa the spirits of the waters are, simply said, snakes. As they are symbolic of healing, they are also believed to "call" to healers to whom they give wisdom and knowledge.[136] According to anthropologist Penny Bernard, "the water spirits have been attributed a pivotal role in the calling, initiation and final induction of certain diviners in the Eastern Cape. Hence the implication that they are the key to certain forms of 'sacred' knowledge." [137]

Tornadoes and waterspouts were believed to be the physical appearance of the African serpent god Inkanyamba. Inkanyamba was believed to be an enormous serpent that twisted and writhed to and fro as it reached from the earth to the sky. Tamra Andrews noted that the Zulu "believed that he grew larger and larger as he rose out of his pool and then grew smaller and smaller when he retreated back into it." [138]

In other African cultures, the snake is considered the spirit of a departed human. Referred to as the 'living-dead' the snake is

---

[134] Budge, E.A. Wallis. *Babylonian Life and History.* New York: Barnes & Noble Books 2005, 167.
[135] Ibid.
[136] Bernard, Penny. "Mermaids, Snakes and the Spirits of the Water in Southern Africa: Implications for River Health", op cit., 3.
[137] Ibid., 4.
[138] Andrews, op cit, 96.

prohibited from being killed, as it is representative of the soul of a relative or friend that is visiting the land of the living. [139]

According to Sumatran and Norse mythology, the vast Cosmic Snake that encircles the world in the cosmic river will eventually destroy it. However from the destruction comes a new world, a renewal of life. The old gods die with the Cosmic Serpent but "Earth will rise again from the waves, fertile, green, and fair as never before, cleansed of all its sufferings and evil."[140]

Perhaps in no other culture than Egypt was the serpent-god so prevalent. The serpent represented both male and female deities, both benign and malevolent. The snake-god Apophis was believed to have existed before time in the primeval chaos of pre-creation. Apophis was the enemy of the sun god and attacked the heavenly ship of Ra as it sojourned across the heavens. The daily battle involved other gods, including Seth the enemy of Osiris, in a back and forth struggle of power between light and dark and balance and chaos. Each day Apophis was defeated, cut into pieces that would revive and rejoin the struggle the next day. In his own way Apophis was a symbol of renewal—renewal brought about by the eternal conflict of the powers of the universe. Apophis was associated with natural disaster, storms, earthquakes and unnatural darkness that foretold the return of chaos. As archaeologist Richard Wilkinson wrote, "Although the god was

---

[139] Mbiti, John S. *African Religions and Philosophy.* Garden City: Anchor Books 1970, 216.

[140] Davidson, H. R. Ellis. *Gods and Myths of the Viking Age.* New York: Bell Publishing Company 1981, 38.

neither worshipped in a formal cult nor incorporated into popular veneration, Apophis entered both spheres of religion as a god or demon to be protected against." [141]

The Egyptians worshiped ten other snake gods. These include Mehen who helped protect Ra from the daily attacks of Apophis, Denwen who was very much like a dragon and had the ability to cause a fiery conflagration, Kebehwet who was a "celestial serpent," Meretseger called the "goddess of the pyramidal peak" and who presided over the necropolis at Thebes. Meretseger became an important deity of the workmen who constructed the burial temples and chambers and many representations of this serpent goddess have been found in workmen's homes and shops in the area.

Other serpent gods of the Egyptians include Nehebu-Kau, "he who harnesses the spirits." [142] Nehebu-Kau was regarded as a helpful deity and was the son of the scorpion goddess Serket. He was referred to in hieroglyph as the "great serpent, multitudinous of coils" and was sometimes depicted as a man with a serpents head. Other beneficent serpent gods include Renenutet, a guardian of the king and goddess of the harvest and fertility. She was also known as a divine nurse. The cobra goddess Wadjet ("the green one") was a goddess of the Nile Delta and was associated with the world of the living rather than the world of the dead. Wadjet was another protector of the king and had

---

[141] Wilkinson, Richard H. *The Complete Gods and Goddesses of Ancient Egypt.* New York: Thames & Hudson 2003, 223.
[142] Ibid, 224.

the ability to spit flames as a defensive measure. The serpent on the pharaoh's crown was that of Wadjet. Like Renenutet, Wadjet was also a nurse to the god Hathor while he was yet a divine infant. Another fiery serpent is Wepset. Wepset, meaning "she who burns," guarded the king, other gods and the Eye of Ra. It was written in ancient texts that the Egyptian island of Biga was her cult center.

The last two Egyptian serpent deities are Weret-Hekau and Yam. "Great of magic" was the name for Weret-Hekau and she may be a composite of other serpent goddesses in that she was also a nursing serpent of the kings and her symbol is associated with the other uraeus goddesses. Yam was actually a Semitic god, a "tyrannical, monstrous deity of the sea", according to Wilkinson.[143] Sometimes depicted as a seven-headed sea monster, Yam was a minor Egyptian god that may have been feared mostly by sailors and fishermen than by regular people of the cities. Yam was defeated in various myths by the goddess Astarte, and the Canaanite god Baal and the Egyptian god Seth.

Serapis, a deity of both the Greeks and Egyptians, associated with Osiris, Hermes, and Hades, was introduced in the 3rd century BCE as a state god for both Greeks and Egyptians. Believed by the Egyptians to be a human manifestation of Apis, a sacred bull that symbolized Osiris, he was represented as a god of fertility and medicine and the ruler of the dead to the Greeks. Serapis was also depicted as a Sun god

---

[143] Ibid, 228.

and occasionally with a serpent wrapped around his body—most likely in connection with fertility.

Serapis

That serpents were, and still are an extremely important aspect of religious traditions around the world cannot be doubted when even Ireland, a land totally devoid of snakes, is so obsessed with the image of the serpent. "Is it not a singular circumstance," said 19th century scholar Marcus Keane, "that in Ireland where no living serpent exists, such numerous legends of serpents should abound, and that figures of serpents should be so profusely used to ornament Irish sculptures?" [144] Celtic scholar James Bonwick himself noted when he visited Cashel,

[144] As quoted by James Bonwick in *Irish Druids and Old Irish Religions.* New York: Barnes & Noble Books 1986, 173. A reprint of the 1894 edition.

Ireland in the 1880's that he saw "a remarkable stone, bearing a nearly defaced sculpture of a female—head and bust—but whose legs were snakes." [145] It was Bonwick's belief that this ancient stone carving depicted an "object of former worship." The "popularity" of the serpent image in Ireland caused Bonwick to write, "That one of the ancient military symbols of Ireland should be a serpent, need not occasion surprise in us. The Druidical serpent or Ireland is perceived in the Tara brooch, popularize to the present day. Irish crosses, so to speak, were alive with serpents." [146]

Serpents were valued in Slavic countries up through the 19th century as good-luck symbols. Snakes were also valued as protective charms in Sweden where they were buried under the foundations of houses and other structures. Russian peasants kept them as pets and, as in Poland; snakes were given food and drink in exchange for their protective charms.

Snakes were associated with an ancient god of thunder in Slavic countries. The thunder god was "responsible for creating mountains and for hurling down bolts of lightning also launched storms of life-giving rain into the earth beneath him." [147] Kerrigan writes "Awesome as his strength was, pagan belief did not characterize it as being

---

[145] Ibid 174.
[146] Ibid 168.
[147] Kerrigan, Michael. "A Fierce Menagerie" in *Forests of the Vampire: Slavic Myth.* New York: Barnes & Noble 2003, 124.

wielded destructively: only with the coming of Christianity did his powers become identified with those of evil." [148]

In some Native American lore, the snake was usually considered an animal to be avoided—one of the "bad animals" that was prohibited from journeying to the spirit world after death. [149] To the Lakota the spirit of the snake "presided over the ability to do things slyly, to go about unknown and unseen, and of lying."[150]

Cherokee shamans prohibited the killing of snakes and the Apache forbid the killing of any snake by their own people but would not hesitate to ask strangers to kill them.[151] The Cherokee generic name for the snake is *inădû'* and they are believed to be supernatural, having close associations with rain and the thunder gods, as well as having a certain influence over other plants and animals. "The feeling toward snakes," wrote James Mooney, "is one of mingled fear and reverence, and every precaution is taken to avoid killing or offending one…"[152] Certain shamans were able to kill rattlesnakes for use in rituals or for medicinal uses. The head was always cut off and buried an arms length

---

[148] Ibid.
[149] Walker, James R. *Lakota Belief and Ritual.* Lincoln: University of Nebraska Press 1991, 71.
[150] Ibid, 122.
[151] Bourke, John G. *Apache Medicine-Men.* New York: Dover Publications, Inc. 1993, 20. A reprint of the1892 edition of *The Medicine-Men of the Apache* published in the Ninth Annual Report of the Bureau of Ethnology to the Secretary of the Smithsonian Institution 1887-88, Washington, pgs 443-603.
[152] Mooney, James. *Myths of the Cherokee.* New York: Dover Publications 1995, 294.

deep in the earth. If this was not done, the snake would cause the rain to fall until the streams and rivers overflowed their banks. [153]

Specific snake lore of the Cherokee indicates that some serpents were not only associated with rain, thunder and the supernatural but also were very unlucky. Mooney reported that a large serpent was once said to reside on the north bank of the Little Tennessee and the main Tennessee rivers in Loudon county, Tennessee and it was considered an evil omen simply to see it. "On one occasion," he wrote, "a man crossing the river…saw the snake in the water and soon afterward lost one of his children." [154]

Illnesses were often thought to be caused by snakes, and even the act of accidentally touching the discarded skin of a snake was believed to cause sickness, especially skin ailments and perhaps even death. [155]

The Apache avoided even mentioning the snake but would sometimes use it as an invective. However, by doing even this one courted disaster. According to Opler, "If a man says in anger, 'I hope a snake bites you,' he will get sick from snakes. ..Before this the snakes have not bothered him, but…it's bound to make him sick." [156]

When a snake is accidentally encountered on a trail, it is, according to Opler, "accorded the greatest respect and is referred to by a

---

[153] Ibid, 296.
[154] Mooney, op cit 414.
[155] Opler, Morris Edward. *An Apache Life-Way: The Economic, Social, and Religious Institutions of the Chiricahua Indians.* Chicago: The University of Chicago Press 1941, 228.
[156] Ibid.

relationship term: …"My mother's father, don't bother me! I'm a poor man. Go where I can't see you. Keep out of my path." [157]

Cherokee lore tells of strange snake-like creatures that were obviously more than myth as no tale of heroes or supernatural interventions are part of the tales. They are simply told as observations and accounts of frightful encounters between men and monster. One such beast is called the Ustû'tlĭ, or "foot snake" which lived on the Cohutta Mountain. Ethnologist James Mooney recorded stories at the beginning of the 20th century about this monster and gives us the following description:

"…it did not glide like other snakes, but had feet at each end of its body, and moved by strides or jerks, like a great measuring worm. These feet were three-cornered and flat and could hold on to the ground like suckers. It had no legs, but would raise itself up on its hind feet, with its snaky head waving high in the air until it found a good place to take a fresh hold…It could cross rivers and deep ravines by throwing its head across and getting a grip with its front feet and then swinging it body over." [158]

A similar creature called the "bouncer" (Uw'tsûñ'ta) lived on the Nantahala River in North Carolina. It too moved by "jerks like a measuring worm." According to lore, this snake like animal was so immense that it would darken the valleys between rifts as it moved across them. According to Mooney the Indians that lived in this area,

---

[157] Ibid, 227.

[158] Mooney, op cit 1995, 302.

fearing the snake eventually deserted the land, "even while still Indian country." [159]

Another monstrous snake, called the Uktena, was said to be as large as a tree trunk with horns on its head. To be able to kill the Uktena enabled the Uktena slayer to obtain a transparent scale from the snake, said to be similar to a crystal that was located on its forehead. To have one was to be blessed with excellent hunting, success in love, rainmaking and life prophecy.

Some Native American people viewed the snake in another way entirely. It was symbolic of the war-god who also had powers over crops and vegetation. "As the emblem of the fertilizing summer showers the lightning serpent was the god of fruitfulness," wrote Lewis Spence, "but as the forerunner of floods and disastrous rains it was feared and dreaded." [160]

That pre-historic Indians believed that the serpent form contained supernatural powers can be surmised by the various serpent mounds constructed in the American heartland. Three such mounds are those found in Adams County, Ohio, St. Peter's River, Iowa and another serpentine mound which extends in sections over two miles in length, also in Iowa. The Great Serpent Mound located in Adams County, Ohio is believed to be the largest serpent effigy in the world at over one-quarter of a mile in length and depicts a serpent in the act of

---

[159] Ibid, 304.

[160] Spence, Lewis. *North American Indians Myths & Legends.* London: Senate 1994, 112. A reprint of *North American Indians* published 1914 by George G. Harrap & Company Ltd.

uncoiling.[161] This unusual earthwork shows the serpent with an egg, perhaps the Cosmic Egg, in its mouth. The culture that created the Great Serpent Mound is unknown since no manmade artifact has been found in connection with the site, although Adena artifacts consisting of copper breastplates, stone points and axes, and grooved sandstone have been found within 400 feet of the mound.

South West American Indian petroglyph of the snake with the cosmic egg.

---

[161] Silverberg, Robert. *Mound Builders of Ancient America: The Archaeology of a Myth.* Greenwich: New York Graphic Society Ltd. 1968, 249.

American folklore has a number of superstitions surrounding the snake. Among these is the notion that a snake cannot cross a horsehair rope but that horsehair placed in a bucket of water will turn into a snake. "A spotted serpent called the milk snake," reports folklorist Vance Randolph, "is said to live by milking cows in the pasture. I know several persons who swear they have seen these snakes sucking milk cows, and they say that a cow which has been milked by a snake is always reluctant to allow a human being to touch her thereafter." [162]

While the snake was often feared, American "hill folk" also respected it. According to Randolph, rather than say the word "snake," like the Apache, "they say 'look out for *our friends* down that way,' or 'there's a lot of *them old things* between here and the river.'" [163]

British folklore says, "if you wear a snake skin round your head, you will never have a headache" and "snakes never die until the sun goes down, however much they may be cut in pieces." [164] However, "if you kill one its mate will come looking for you." [165]Another advises that to stay young—eat snake!

---

[162] Randolph, Vance. *Ozark Magic and Folklore.* New York: Dover Publications, Inc. 1964, 257. A reprint of the 1947 edition of *Ozark Superstitions* published by Columbia University Press.
[163] Ibid, 258.
[164] Radford, Edwin and Mona A. *Encyclopaedia of Superstitions.* New York: Philosophical Library 1949, 221.
[165] Simpson, Jacqueline and Steve Roud. *Oxford Dictionary of English Folklore.* Oxford: Oxford University Press 2000, 2.

In 19th century Gaelic folklore the serpent is more evil than good. Campbell wrote, "A serpent, whenever encountered, ought to be killed. Otherwise, the encounter will prove an evil omen.

"The head should be completely smashed…and removed to a distance from the rest of the body. Unless this is done the serpent will again come alive. The tail, unless deprived of animation, will join the body, and the head becomes a *beithir,* the largest and most deadly kind of serpent." [166]

In other cultures, like many Native American ones, there is a prohibition against killing snakes. Frazer wrote "In Madras it is considered a great sin to kill a cobra. When this has happened, the people generally burn the body of the serpent, just as they burn the bodies of human beings. The murderer deems himself polluted for three days."[167] In other areas of the world, snakes were annually sacrificed in large numbers by burning. This occurred at Luchon in the Pyrenees on Midsummer Eve at least into the early 20th century. Considered a Pagan survival, the ritual was led by the local clergy. Frazer describes the event:

"At an appointed hour—about 8 PM—a grand procession, composed of the clergy, followed by young men and maidens in holiday attire, pour forth from the town chanting hymns, and take up their position [around a wicker-work column raised 60 feet in height].

---

[166] Campbell, John Gregorson. *The Gaelic Otherworld,* edited by Ronald Black. Edinburgh: Birlinn Limited 2005, 121.

[167] Frazer, Sir James. *The Golden Bough: A study in magic and religion.* Hertfordshire: Wordsworth Editions 1993, 222.

...bonfires are lit, with beautiful effect, in the surrounding hills. As many living serpents as could be collected are now thrown into the column, which is set on fire at the base by means of torches, armed with which about fifty boys and men dance around with frantic gestures. The serpents...wriggle their way to the top...until finally obliged to drop, their struggles for life giving rise to enthusiastic delight among the surrounding spectators." [168]

Serpents have been mercilessly hunted and killed by many cultures the world over but it is possible, according to Jyoti Sahi, that "all religions which have evolved the concept of a really personal god...have emerged out of a tradition in which serpents have been extremely important symbols of the supernatural." [169]

Hecate and the Cat

The cat has long been one of humankinds favored animals. It has been worshipped as a god by the Egyptians and feared as a demon by Christians terrified by witchcraft. It is both a beloved family pet and a fierce feral predator. It is a loving companion but never tamed. Like most symbols universally important in societies around the world, the cat has a dual nature of both good and evil aspects.

One of Hecate's shape-shifting forms is that of the cat. According to Howey, "...the cat was the chosen transformation of the great Diana (or Hecate) herself in her hour of peril, when the terrible Typhon forced the gods to hide their divinity in animal shapes, and

[168] Ibid 655-656.
[169] Sahi, op cit 166.

flee into Egypt." [170] Black cats are symbolic of the moon, mystery and death—all aspects of Hecate in her various forms. Plutarch wrote that the cat, who was often depicted with the crescent moon on its head, "was the proper emblem of the moon" of which Hecate was the ruler.

Prior to the advent of Christianity, the Old Religion was undergoing radical changes. "Luna, Diana, and Hecate were torn asunder," wrote Howey, "and no more seen as the triple aspects of the one Great Mother. There was war in Heaven." [171] Sorcery in the ancient times was viewed as a sacred art, the sorcerer the possessor of magical knowledge given by the gods. The Old Religion, Howey noted, "had been misinterpreted and cruelly degraded." [172] The cat was involved in this process and suffered greatly because of it. "Perhaps because of its nocturnal habits," Howey wrote, "the Cat from ancient times had been considered the most acceptable offering to the gods of darkness, and the subterranean deities. To sacrifice a cat was a sure means on contacting these deities, and persuading them to confer the gift of second sight, which the Cat, as their representative, was believed to possess.

"But," Howey continues, "as the idea of forcing the gods gained ground, the Cat sacrifice was newly interpreted. The gods loved the Cat as their chosen and sacred symbol. To torture it mercilessly would be to oblige them to grant any request that its persecutor made the

---

[170] Howey, M. Oldfield. *The Cat in Magic, Mythology, and Religion.* New York: Crescent Books 1989, 96.
[171] Ibid. 109.
[172] Ibid. 110.

condition of its release. Here was an invincible weapon that the strong and unscrupulous might wield." [173]

It was during this radical change in the Old Religion that Christianity arose. Christians were taught that all gods and goddesses not part of Christianity were evil and must be destroyed. Because the cat was an important symbol of the Old Religion, it too was subject to the cruelties of the new religion.

The Egyptian cat-goddess Bast

Like the dog, the cat has a long history in folklore, mythology, and ancient religions. Cats represent clairvoyance, watchfulness, mystery,

[173] Ibid., 111.

female malice and sensual beauty. In India, it was believed that cats could take over the bodies of women at will. [174] On the other hand, the Indian goddess of maternity and protector of children, Sasti, is a feline goddess that rides on a cat. [175]

Both Chinese and Japanese folklore views the cat as symbolic of transformation. Scandinavian mythology says that the goddess Freyja's chariot is drawn by cats. In Egyptian mythology the goddess Bast, the moon goddess, is cat-headed and the cat also symbolized the protective aspects of the Mother Goddess, Isis.

In Cambodia, the cat is associated with drought and is carried in cages to rain ravaged areas where it is doused with water. It is believed that the cat's howls will awaken the rain goddess Indra so that she will stop the downpour. [176]

Big cats have dominated the ancient religious traditions of Mesoamerica. Appearing as a jaguar or puma or as a composite jaguar human figure, the cat gods were associated with caves, the night and the underworld. Much as cats had been viewed during the witch-hunting days of Europe.

One of the main deities of the Olmec people was the were-jaguar, half human and half jaguar the were-jaguar was important for its rain making abilities. The Maya had the most jaguar deities than any other

---

[174] Tresidder, Jack. *Symbols and Their Meanings.* London: Duncan Baird Publishers 2000, 59.

[175] Mackenzie, Donald A. *Myths and Legends: India.* London: Studio Editions 1985, 153.

[176] Keister, Douglas. *Stories in Stone.* New York: MJF Books 2004, 71.

Mesoamerican people. They regarded the jaguar as representative of the sun. Miller and Taube noted that the Mayan jaguar was the nighttime sun, and as god of the Underworld it was also the Underworld's sun. [177] The jaguar image is frequently associated with sacrifice.

Black cats are normally thought to bring bad luck—except in England where they have the opposite effect. Images of black cats in England are made into good luck charms. Symbologist J. C. Cooper, however, noted, "As black it is lunar, evil and death; it is only in modern times that a black cat has been taken to signify good luck." [178] Ancient Chinese tradition speaks of the black cat as representative of misfortune and, of course, Christian symbolism links the black cat with Satan, lust, laziness and witchcraft.

While cats have caused some fear among humans for their mystical character it is the cat that has paid the price more than their human companions have. According to an entry in the January 11, 1851 *Notes and Queries* British periodical, "In Wilts, and also in Devon, it is believed that cats born in the Month of May will catch no mice nor rats, but will, contrary to the wont of other cats, bring in snakes and slow worms. Such cats are called 'May cats,' and are held in contempt." [179] "May cats" seem to have been universally disliked in England in the

---

[177] Miller, Mary and Karl Taube. *The Gods and Symbols of Ancient Mexico and the Maya.* London: Thames and Hudson 1993, 104.
[178] Cooper, J.C. *An Illustrated Encyclopaedia of Traditional Symbols.* London: Thames and Hudson 1978. 30
[179] *Notes and Queries*, Vol. 3, Number 63, January 11, 1851, 20.

19th century. Another *Notes and Queries* entry on February 1, 1851 stated "In Hampshire, to this day, we always kill may cats," and in June another reader wrote "…may Cats are unlucky, and will suck the breath of children." [180] This last superstition is still commonly found in the Western world.

Cats are also invariably linked to the weather—and generally not good weather. The approach of wind and rain was said to be foretold by the way a cat washes itself or in what direction it sits while grooming. Greek folklore from the 1890's said "…if a cat licks herself with her face turned towards the north, the wind will soon blow from that dangerous quarter." [181] Witch-lore says that the cat familiar is a rain-maker as well as a companion to the witch. Foretelling the weather by watching a cat may not be foolproof however. Another bit of weather-lore says "Cats with their tails up and hair apparently electrified indicate approaching wind, --or a dog." [182]

Witches have long been associated with the cat—the cat being either the witches familiar or a form that the witch easily transforms into. This relationship is an ancient one, the Greeks and Romans told of a woman who had been changed into a cat chosen as the priestess of Hecate, goddess of the Underworld, sorcery and magic. In fact, Hecate is often depicted as a cat. It is interesting that the cat is so universally thought of in this manner as, in reality, there are more

---

[180] *Notes and Queries*, Vol. 3, Number 87, June 28, 1851, 516.
[181] Inwards, Richard. *Weather Lore.* London: Elliot Stock 1893, 126.
[182] Ibid.

stories of rabbits being associated with witches than the cat. While there is some court testimony of the 16th century concerning witches shape-shifting into cats, many other animals were also implicated such as dogs, frogs, cocks and hares. In 1587 twenty-four Aberdeen witches were tried and eventually "They accused one another of unnatural practices, from eating mutton on Good Friday to concourse with devils in the shape of black cats and dogs." [183]

This belief in witches assuming the form of cats was not restricted to Europe by any means. Folklorist Vance Randolph wrote in his 1947 study, *Ozark Superstitions* that "A witch can assume the form of any bird or animal, but cats and wolves seem to be her favorite disguises. In many a backwoods village you may hear some gossip about a woman who visits her lover in the guise of a house cat. Once inside his cabin, she assumes her natural form and spends the night with him. Shortly before daybreak she becomes a cat again, returns to her home, and is transformed into a woman at her husband's beside." [184]

In popular folklore, the witch was said to be able to assume the form of a black cat nine times—to match the nine magical lives that the cat is supposedly blessed with. Across Medieval Europe, black cats

---

[183] Parrinder, Geoffry. "The Witch as Victim" in *The Witch in History* edited by Venetia Newall. New York: Barnes & Noble 1996, 129.

[184] Randolph, Vance. *Ozark Magic and Folklore.* New York: Dover Publications, Inc. 1964, 268. A reprint of *Ozark Superstitions* published 1947 by Columbia University Press.

were hunted down and killed—usually by burning. This most often occurred on Shrove Tuesday [185] and Easter.

In fact, notes Thompson, "the connection of the cat with witches was no doubt the reason for the persecution and ill-treatment of the animal in the seventeenth century." [186]

Cats have been fearfully linked to death, probably as a result of their association with the witch trials but also due to their ties to ancient predator animal deities around the world and to ancient gods and goddesses of the Underworld.

In Estonian folklore, the returning souls of dead humans, called "home wanderers," or "revenants" could appear in human or animal form. According to Estonian folklorist Eha Viluoja, out of 92 reported instances of "home wanderer" observations, cats (black of course) accounted for 17 of them. Dogs were the primary ghostly object seen, accounting for 35 cases. [187]

Any cat that jumped over a body awaiting burial was a sure sign of bad luck and immediately killed. It was believed that should a cat do such a thing the corpse would rise up to become a vampire.[188]

---

[185] Shrove Tuesday is the last day before Lent. It was a day that became popular for divination among many other activities.

[186] Thompson, C.J.S. *The Hand of Destiny.* New York: Bell Publishing Company 1989, 201.

[187] Viluoja, Eha. "Manifestations of the Revenant in Estonian Folk Tradition", in Folklore, Vol. 2. http://www.folklore.ee/folklore/vol2/viluoja.htm 8/14/06

[188] Guiley, Rosemary Ellen. *The Encyclopedia of Witches & Witchcraft.* New York: Checkmark Books/Facts on File 1999, 49

Regardless if the cat is empowered with evil forces; it has been used to affect folk-cures and to provide protection—in rather strange ways. Folklorist Luc Lacourcière noted that in French Canada it was not uncommon to attempt to transfer disease from the human patient to an animal. In the case of shingles, a skinned-cat was applied to the human body so that the disease could be absorbed into the body of the dead cat.[189] Other treatments include making the sign of the cross with a cat's tail over an eye afflicted with a sty. This reportedly will make the sty disappear. This treatment was used in such diverse areas as Louisiana and England. [190] It was not reported if the cat was living or dead when its tail was used for this purpose. A broth, made from a black cat, was also consumed to cure consumption.

The mystic power of the cat was continuously sought until well into the 19th and 20th century and, most likely, into the 21st century as well. Folk-medicine practices around the world abound in strange rituals to cure certain diseases or to warn individuals away from potentially dangerous events. Many of these today seem naïve and childish—as well as cruel for the poor animals involved. In Oregon in the 1960's folklore warned, "Never allow a child to play with cats or he will become a simpleton." A similar prohibition was reported in Ohio

---

[189] Lacourcière, Luc. "A Survey of Folk Medicine in French Canada from Early Times to the Present", in *American Folk Medicine*, edited by Wayland D. Hand. Berkeley: University of California Press 1976, 212.

[190] Simpson, Jacqueline and Steve Roud. *Oxford Dictionary of English Folklore.* Oxford: Oxford University Press 2000, 50 and Elizabeth Brandon. "Folk Medicine in French Louisiana" in *American Folk Medicine.* Edited by Wayland D. Hand. Berkeley: University of California Press 1976, 200.

in the 1950's, "If a boy plays with cats, it will make him stupid, for the cat's brain will go into him." [191]

Other dangers associated with playing with cats include the very real possibility of women becoming pregnant (recorded in Oslo during the 1930's). While some folklore warns against being overly friendly with cats the obverse was also true during the 1950's in the American Mid-West. "If you make enemies of cats during your lifetime," it was reported, "you will be accompanied to the grave by storms of wind and rain." [192]

Other folk-medicine traditions include one from Germany during the early 20th century that said that thieves could become invisible by cutting off the tips of the tongue of black cats and dogs, "wrap them in wax of an Easter candle, and carry them under the left arm." [193]

A rather grisly tradition in Christian England included sacrificing a cat to ward off evil forces when buildings were constructed. Originally cats, and other animals as well as humans in pre-historic times, were killed and buried in building foundations as sacrifices to the gods and spirits to ensure protection of the structure. Over time, the "sacrificial" aspect was rationalized. Archaeologist Ralph Merrifield wrote, "the cruel practice of killing a cat as a builder's sacrifice was revived by the notion that the body of a cat set in a lifelike attitude in a hidden place

---

[191] UCLA Folkmedicine Record Numbers 10_4587, 11_4890.

[192] Ibid, Record Number 5_5244

[193] Hoffman-Krayer, Eduard von and Hanns Bächtold-Stäubli, eds. *Handwörterbuch des deutschen Aberglaubens.* Berlin & Leipzig 1927-1942, vol. 2, 235.

would frighten vermin from the building." [194] What the actual "vermin" were is questionable however. Were rodents the focus of these efforts or was it more the spiritual "rodent"—demons and witches—that were the objects of such fear? In some instances, a dead cat was found with a single rat in its mouth or near a paw.

While this use of "charms" was widespread across England, from the 15th to 19th centuries it also occurred in other locations such as Gibraltar and Sweden.

The Horse

Many images of Hecate showing her in her tri-form aspect depict her with a head of a dog, a snake and a horse. Like Hecate the horse is a life and death symbol—representing both the illuminating sun and the moon. And, like Hecate the horse represented wisdom, reason, nobility and magical powers such as contained in the winds and the waves of the ocean.

The horse is sacred to many gods and goddesses. Epona of the Celts, Poseidon, Apollo and Mithra. It is sacred as well to Diana and Odin and carried thunderbolts for Zeus.

---

[194] Merrifield, Ralph. *The Archaeology of Ritual and Magic.* New York: New Amsterdam Books 1987, 186

Six
Plants Sacred to Hecate

As the mythic creator of herbal medicines and poisons there would naturally be a number of plants sacred to Hecate. Among the trees sacred to this goddess are the yew, willow, cypress, hazel, cedar and black poplar.

Herbs and plants that were associated with her include garlic, thyme, almonds, myrrh, mugwort, mint, dandelion, cardamon, hellbore, lesser celandine and poisonous and hallucinogenic plants such as belladonna, hemlock, mandrake, hecateis (aconite) and the opium poppy.

The yew tree is sacred in many cultures. The yew also symbolizes death and, in fact, a potion made from yew seeds was applied to arrows, which could cause death. Yew berries were also used as a poison but were also said to bestow wisdom.

The yew has been known as the "death tree" in all European countries. The yew may also figure in the creation of the Green Man. "In Brittany", Graves writes, "it is said that church-yard yews will spread a root to the mouth of each corpse." [195] The yew was also one of the Five Magical Trees of Ireland.

The yew is not a death tree in that it causes death, although some lore does suggest that death will soon follow if certain yews are

---

[195] Graves, Robert. *The White Goddess.* New York: The Noonday Press 1948, 194.

irreverently plucked, rather it is regarded as a "gentle guardian of the dead." The yew has been a common churchyard tree for this reason. In Wales, it was sacrilegious to burn or cut down a yew. [196] The yews association with death made it an unlucky tree that was not to be taken into the home.

The yew is another of those trees with a dual symbolism. While it represented mourning and sadness, it also symbolized, for Christians and Celts, immortality. As researcher Gale Owen writes, "The yew-tree can be either an optimistic or a pessimistic symbol; as an evergreen its branches might be used in winter fertility ceremonies as a reminder of rebirth. Yet its leaves are very dark…to the Romans the yew was associated with poison and death." [197] The yew was also one of two trees that the Druids utilized for their wands—the other being the rowan. The usage of yew in the making of power wands was common around the world. The "power sticks" of the Tillamook shamans along the Oregon coast were also made of yew.

The yew, as with the other sacred trees and plants, was utilized in treating illnesses and injuries as well. Seventeenth century treatments for heart palpitations and included the use of yew berries. Czech folklorist Josef Cizmár noted in "some regions, blessed twigs of yew-tree are used in smoking cures of eye ailments" [198] and the sawdust of

---

[196] Radford, Edwin and Mona A. *Encyclopaedia of Superstitions.* New York: The Philosophical Library 1949, 264.

[197] Owen, Gale R. *Rites and Religions of the Anglo-Saxons.* Dorset Press 1985, 56

[198] Cizmár, Josef. *Lidové lékarství v Ceskoslovensku. Vol. 2*. Czechoslovakia: Melantrich, A.S. 1946, 200

yew was used as a cure for rabies. Another remedy for rabies involved a rather complex ceremony involving cooking and ritual:

"One has to boil savory and yew, to mix in the extract rye flour (after cooling), and cut in the dough a little bit of window lead. Then three cakes should be baked of the mixture, and the ill one should eat them on an empty stomach. After prayers (Lord Prayer and Ave Maria said five times; Credo, one time), he should offer everything to the Five Wounds of Jesus Christ." [199]

The willow was one of the symbols of the goddess Hecate in her virgin form. It is an enchanted tree sacred to the Moon Goddess, Europa, Kwan-yin, Artemis, Hera, Tammuz, and Esus. A willow was the Cosmic Tree of Accadia. Willow wands figured prominently in the rituals of several Middle Eastern religions, including that of Dionysus, and were incorporated in the Day of Willows feast, later known as the Feast of the Tabernacle. [200] Willow was also favored as a source wood for the construction of divining rods due to the magical properties it supposedly contained. These rods not only led one to hidden treasures but also drive away the "powers of darkness, serpents, and other evils."[201] Cooper notes that it is especially sacred to the Ainu "since the spine of the first man was made of willow." [202] The village hedge witch

---

[199] Ibid. 44.
[200] Walker, Barbara G. *The Women's Encyclopedia of Myths and Secrets.* Edison: Castle Books 1996, 1076.
[201] Porteous, Alexander. *The Lore of the Forest.* London: Senate 1996, 262
[202] Cooper, J.C. *An Illustrated Encyclopaedia on Traditional Symbols.* London: Thames and Hudson Ltd. 1978, 192.

used willow bark to treat fevers and arthritis, which was effective due to its aspirin qualities. However, according to lore, animals struck with a willow rod "will be seized with internal pains" [203] and children struck with it were said to stop growing.

The willow is also associated with magic. Because it naturally grows near water it is believed to mark the entrance to the underworld. Its ancient ties to the witch are indicated by the origins of the name. "Willow" is a derivative of the Old English word *wicce*, whereby "wicker" is another derivative. Contemporary witches are often called "Wiccans."

The Cypress was another tree long associated with death. It was also believed to have the power to preserve the deceased body from decay so it was often used for burials. As other symbols, the Cypress had a dual nature. It was an emblem of Zeus, Apollo, Hermes and Venus and symbolized life but as it was associated with the gods of the underworld it signified death and fate as well.

The cedar, while not part of the Celtic ogham script, was a sacred tree in many lands and many cultures. The cedar was closely associated with the Accadian-Chaldean god Ea, whose name, tradition says, was inscribed on the core, or heart, of the tree. To the Chaldeans the cedar not only represented the god Ea, "the god of wisdom", but also

---

[203] Burns, Charlotte Sophia. *The Handbook of Folklore*. London: Senate 1996, 32 (A reprint of the 1914 edition published by Sidgwick & Jackson Ltd., London)

reflected the divine power actually inherent in the tree. [204] To the Chaldeans the cedar of Ea was a divine oracle. In India, the cedar was believed to be a great aid in the fertility of cattle and women alike.

To the Sumerians the cedar was the Cosmic Tree and the Tree of Life. It was also sacred to the Green God Tammuz and, as all sacred trees do, had magical properties. The cedar represents strength, nobility, and incorruptibility. [205]

Native Americans also universally regarded the cedar as sacred. It was an important part of the Ghost Dance religion of the Sioux in the late 1800s, standing tall as the sacrificial pole in the rituals of that religion. The Ghost Dance, a Native American revivalist-messianic movement, itself was performed around a small cedar tree planted in the ground specifically for that reason. "The selection of the cedar", wrote ethnologist James Mooney in 1896, "…is in agreement with the general Indian idea, which has always ascribed a mystic sacredness to that tree, from its never-dying green, which renders it so conspicuous a feature of the desert landscape; from the aromatic fragrance of its twigs, which are burned as incense in sacred ceremonies…and from the dark-red color of its heart, which seems as though dyed in blood."[206]

---

[204] Philpot, Mrs. J. H. *The Sacred Tree in Religion and Myth.* Mineola: Dover Publications Inc. 2004, 95 (A reprint of the 1897 edition published by Macmillan and Co. Ltd, New York & London)

[205] Cooper, op cit, 31

[206] Moony, James. *The Ghost-Dance Religion and the Sioux Outbreak of 1890.* Chicago: The University of Chicago Press 1965, 53 (A reprint of Part 2 of the

According to Mooney, the cedar incense was so potent that malevolent ghosts are unable to endure it and are driven away by its fragrance, even though "the wood itself is considered too sacred to be used as fuel." [207]

In Cherokee mythology, the red color of the cedar is from the blood of a wizard slain and decapitated by a Cherokee warrior. The wizard's head, according to the myth, was hung from several trees but continued to live. A shaman told the people to hang the head from the topmost branches of a cedar, where it finally died. [208] In this way, the cedar became a "medicine tree."

The cedar is sacred to the Lakota as it was a special tree of *Wakinyan*, the Flying God, or Thunderbird. In Lakota lore, "the cedar tree is the favorite of *Wakinyan,* and he never strikes it with lightning. The smell of the cedar is pleasing to him." [209] The Lakota lit the cedar incense to propitiate Wakinyan and to keep thunderstorms from causing damage.

The Egyptians also considered the cedar a holy tree. On the Obelisk of Thutmose III, hieroglyphs speak of the creation of the sacred barge of Amun-Ra made from cedar cut down by the pharaoh

---

Fourteenth Annual Report of the Bureau of Ethnology to the Secretary of the Smithsonian Institution, 1892-93. Washington: Government Printing Office 1896)

[207] Mooney, James. *Myths of the Cherokee.* New York: Dover Publications Inc. 1995, 421 (A reprint of the *Nineteenth Annual Report of the Bureau of American Ethnology 1897*-98 published in1900 by the Smithsonian Institution, Washington)

[208] Ibid, 228

[209] Walker, James R. *Lakota Belief and Ritual.* Lincoln: University of Nebraska Press 1991, 77

himself. The barge was ceremoniously sailed down the Nile for the annual river festival. [210]

The cedar tree, like most other sacred trees, has a dual nature. It is at once healing and deadly. Native Americans used cedar to treat asthma, arthritis and even relieve persons in coma. Other American folk-cures used cedar to stop night sweats (accomplished by placing cedar bark or leaves under the pillow), and if one carried a "double cedar knot" in his or her pocket rheumatism was certain to be cured.[211]

On the other side, cedar was often regarded as a source of evil and danger. It was commonly believed in the mid-west and southern parts of the United States that if a planted cedar tree died, so did the owner. Canadian Indian shamans also used cedar as a "soul trap." A piece of netting, made of cedar, was constructed three feet square with a quarter inch mesh to trap a "wandering soul." [212]

Frazer notes that a girl was sacrificed each year to an old cedar in the Kangra Mountains of India. Frazer further noted, "the families of the village taking it in turn to supply the victim." [213] The sacrifice was to appease the spirit of the tree.

---

[210] Budge, E.A. Wallis. *Cleopatra's Needles and Other Egyptian Obelisks.* New York: Dover Publications, Inc. 1990, 156 (A reprint of the 1926 edition published by the Religious Tract Society, London)

[211] Sackett, S.J. "More Folk Medicine from Western Kansas" in *Western Folklore* #23 1964. Published by the California Folklore Society, UCLA, 76

[212] Darby, George E. "Indian Medicine in British Columbia" in *The Canadian Medical Association Journal* #28 1933, 437

[213] Frazer, Sir James. *The Golden Bough: A Study in Magic and Religion.* Hertfordshire: Wordsworth Editions Ltd. 1993, 112

It is, however the evergreen nature of the cedar that invokes its true value—it symbolizes eternal life, and victory over the bindings of death.

Hazel was the sacred tree in the Druid grove, representing wisdom, magic, divination, inspiration and chthonic powers. In England, the hazel was associated with fertility and divination. It was the Celtic Tree of Life and was associated with the Mother Goddess. Hazel nuts would bestow wisdom to those who ate them but only the sacred salmon were allowed to eat them. "All the knowledge of the arts and sciences", wrote Graves "was bound up with the eating of these nuts."[214] The "nine hazels of poetic arts" grew next to the Connla's Well near Tipperary, said to produce both fruit and flowers at the same time. In Scandinavia, the hazel was sacred to Thor. Sacred hazel groves at one time existed near Edinburgh and Glasgow.[215] Hazel was valued for forming powerful wands as well. Called the Wishing, or Diving Rod, it was used in magic and for locating hidden springs and treasure. The hazel was also regarded as a "lightning shrub", acting as a lightning rod it was often attached to door or window frames for a bit of added protection during storms.[216] "Wishing Caps" were once made of hazel twigs and if worn "it is possible to obtain any wish." [217] Ship

---

[214] Graves, op cit 182
[215] Ibid 49
[216] Thompson, C.J.S. *The Hand of Destiny: Everyday Folklore and Superstitions.* London: Senate, 219 (A reprint of the 1932 edition published by Rider & Company, London)
[217] Radford, op cit 145

captains would wear them, as they believed that by doing so their ship could weather any storm.

The poplar is "a tree of the waters." [218] In Greco-Roman mythology, the white poplar (also known as the aspen) represents the Elysian Fields, while the black, according to some, represents Hades, the underworld land of the dead, and Hecate. To be more generous of the black poplar we may say that it was sacred to Mother Earth and was the funereal tree of pre-Hellenic Greece.

Many of the plants mentioned are used by those attempting to enter shamanic trances or ecstatic states, which would have been common for the followers of Hecate as they were for other mystery cults.

---

[218] Cooper, op cit 134

About the Author

Gary R. Varner has written a number of books and articles on folklore, mythology and early religions. He has contributed to a number of scholarly periodicals as well, including *Living Spring Journal* (UK) and *Magister Botanicus* (Germany). He is a member of the American Folklore Society and has been listed in a number of editions of *Who's Who in America* and *Who's Who in the World.*

Books by the author include *Mysteries of Native American Myth and Religion, The Gods of Man – Gods of Nature God of War, Creatures in the Mist: Little People, Wild Men and Spirit Beings Around the World, The Mythic Forest, the Green Man and the Spirit of Nature, Sacred Wells: The History, Meaning and Mythology of Holy Wells and Waters, The Dark Wind: Witches and the Concept of Evil* and *Ghosts, Spirits & the Afterlife in Native American Folklore and Religion.*

Currently living in Northern California, the author invites interested readers to visit him at www.authorsden.com/garyrvarner.

Selected Bibliography

Beckwith, Martha. *Hawaiian Mythology.* Honolulu: University of Hawaii Press 1970

Black, Jeremy and Anthony Green. *Gods, Demons and Symbols of Ancient Mesopotamia.* Austin: University of Texas Press 1992

Briggs, Katherine. *British Folktales.* New York: Pantheon Books 1977

Briggs, Robin. *Witches & Neighbors: The Social and Cultural Context of European Witchcraft.* New York: Viking Press 1996

Campbell, John Gregorson. *The Gaelic Otherworld*, edited by Ronald Black. Edinburgh: Birlinn Ltd. 2005

Cooper, J.C. *An Illustrated Encyclopaedia on Traditional Symbols.* London: Thames and Hudson Ltd. 1978

Crowley, Vivianne. *Phoenix and the Flame: Pagan Spirituality in the Western World.* London: Aquarian/Thorsons 1994

Davidson, H. R. Ellis. *Myths and Symbols in Pagan Europe: Early Scandinavian and Celtic Religions.* Syracuse: Syracuse University Press 1988

Elworthy, Frederick Thomas. *The Evil Eye: An Account of this Ancient and Widespread Superstition.* London: John Murray 1895

Ely, Talfourd. *The Gods of Greece and Rome.* Mineola: Dover Publications, Inc. 2003

Evans-Wentz, W.Y. *The Fairy-Faith in Celtic Countries.* Mineola: Dover Publications Inc. 2002

Fiske, John. *Myths and Myth-Makers: Old Tales and Superstitions Interpreted by Comparative Mythology.* Boston: Houghton, Mifflin and Company 1881

Franklin, Anna. *The Illustrated Encyclopaedia of Fairies.* London: Paper Tiger 2004

Frazer, Sir James. *The Golden Bough: A Study in Magic and Religion.* Hertfordshire: Wordsworth Editions Ltd. 1993

Green, Miranda. *The Gods of the Celts.* Gloucester: Alan Sutton 1986

Guiley, Rosemary Ellen. *The Encyclopedia of Witches & Witchcraft.* New York: Checkmark Books 1999

Hutton, Ronald. *The Pagan Religions of the Ancient British Isles: Their Nature and Legacy.* Oxford: Blackwell Publishers Ltd., 1991

James, E.O. *The Cult of the Mother-Goddess.* New York: Barnes & Noble, Inc. 1994

Johnson, Buffie. *Lady of the Beasts: The Goddess and Her Sacred Animals.* Rochester: Inner Traditions International 1994

Jordan, Katy. *The Haunted Landscape: Folklore, ghosts & legends of Wiltshire.* Wiltshire: Ex Libris Press 2000

Kieckhefer, Richard. *Magic in the Middle Ages.* Cambridge: Cambridge University Press 1989

MacCulloch, J.A. *The Religion of the Ancient Celts.* Mineola: Dover Publications, Inc. 2003

MacKenzie, Donald A. *Ancient Man in Britain.* London: Senate 1996. A reprint of the 1922 edition published by Blackie & Son Ltd, London.

Mackenzie, Donald A. *India Myths & Legends*. London: Studio Editions 1993

Mbiti, John S. *African Religions and Philosophy*. Garden City: Anchor Books 1969

Merrifield, Ralph. *The Archaeology of Ritual and M*agic. New York: New Amsterdam Books 1987

Mohen, Jean-Pierre. *Prehistoric Art: The Mythical Birth of Humanity*. Paris: Pierre Terrail/Telleri 2002

Mooney, James. *Myths of the Cherokee*. New York: Dover Publications Inc. 1995 (A reprint of the *Nineteenth Annual Report of the Bureau of American Ethnology 1897*-98 published in1900 by the Smithsonian Institution, Washington)

Murray, Margaret A. *The Witch-Cult in Western Europe*. Oxford: Oxford University Press 1921

Ogden, Daniel. "Binding Spells: Curse Tablets and Voodoo Dolls in the Greek and Roman World" in *Witchcraft and Magic in Europe: Ancient Greece and Rome*. Ed. by Bengt Ankarloo and Stuart Clark. Philadelphia: University of Pennsylvania Press 1999, pgs 3-90.

Ogden, Daniel. *Magic, Witchcraft, and Ghosts in the Greek and Roman Worlds: A Sourcebook*. Oxford: Oxford University Press 2002

Philips, David E. *Legendary Connecticut: Traditional Tales from the Nutmeg State*. Williamantic: Curbstone Press 1992

Philpot, Mrs. J. H. *The Sacred Tree in Religion and Myth*. Mineola: Dover Publications Inc. 2004 (A reprint of the 1897 edition published by Macmillan and Co. Ltd, New York & London)

Porteous, Alexander. *The Lore of the Forest*. London: Senate 1996

Radford, Edwin and Mona A. *Encyclopaedia of Superstitions*. New York: The Philosophical Library 1949

Randolph, Vance. *Ozark Magic and Folklore*. New York: Dover Publications, Inc. 1964. A reprint of *Ozark Superstitions* published by Columbia University Press 1947.

Russell, Jeffrey Burton. *Witchcraft in the Middle Ages*. Ithaca: Cornell University Press 1972

Sjöö, Monica and Barbara Mor. *The Great Cosmic Mother: Rediscovering the Religion of the Earth*. San Francisco: HarperSanFrancisco 1991

Stapleton, Michael. *Library of the World's Myths and Legends: Greek and Roman Mythology*. New York: Peter Bedrick Books 1986

Titcomb, Margaret. *Dog and Man in the Ancient Pacific*. Honolulu: Bernice P. Bishop Museum Special Publication 59 1969

Trubshaw, Bob. "Black Dogs: Guardians of the corpse ways" in At The Edge, August 2001 http://www.indigogroup.co.uk/edge/bdogs.htm.

Walker, Barbara G. *The Women's Encyclopedia of Myths and Secrets*. Edison: Castle Books 1996

Werner, E.T.C. *Myths and Legends of China*. New York: Dover Publications, Inc. 1994

Westervelt, William D. *Myths and Legends of Hawaii*. Honolulu: Mutual Publishing 1987

Westwood, Jennifer. *Albion: A Guide to Legendary Britain*. London: Paladin/Grafton Books 1985,

White, David Gordon. *Myths of the Dog-Man*. Chicago: University of Chicago Press 1991

Wilbert, Johannes. *Yupa Folktales.* Latin American Studies, Volume 24. Los Angeles: University of California Los Angeles 1974

Zigmond, Maurice L. "The Supernatural World of the Kawaiisu" in Thomas C. Blackburn (ed.) *Flowers of the Wind: Papers on Ritual, Myth, And Symbolism in California and the Southwest.* Socorro: Ballena Press 1977

Note: Portions of Chapter Five appeared in *Creatures in the Mist: Little People, Wild Men and Spirit Beings Around the World* by Gary R. Varner, published by Algora Publishing, New York 2007.

Portions of Chapter Six appeared in *The Mythic Forest, The Green Man and the Spirit of Nature* by Gary R. Varner, published by Algora Publishing 2006.

Index

www.ingramcontent.com/pod-product-compliance
Ingram Content Group UK Ltd.
Pitfield, Milton Keynes, MK11 3LW, UK
UKHW041936190726
13854UKWH00004B/1626